**OGC Portfolio Product**

D0661461

# ITIL® V3 Foundation Handbook

*it*SMF UK
The IT Service Management Forum

London: TSO

information & publishing solutions

Published by TSO (The Stationery Office) and
available from:

**Online**
www.tsoshop.co.uk

**Mail, Telephone, Fax & E-mail**
TSO
PO Box 29, Norwich, NR3 1GN
Telephone orders/General enquiries: 0870
600 5522
Fax orders: 0870 600 5533
E-mail: customer.services@tso.co.uk
Textphone 0870 240 3701

**TSO@Blackwell and other Accredited Agents**

**Customers can also order publications from:**
TSO Ireland
16 Arthur Street, Belfast BT1 4GD
Tel 028 9023 8451 Fax 028 9023 5401

The Swirl logo™ is a Trade Mark of the Office of
Government Commerce

ITIL® is a Registered Trade Mark of the Office of
Government Commerce in the United Kingdom
and other countries

The ITIL endorsement logo™ is a Trade Mark of
the Office of Government Commerce

A CIP catalogue record for this book is available
from the British Library

A Library of Congress CIP catalogue record has
been applied for

First edition 2008

Second edition 2009

First published 2009

ISBN 9780113311972 Single copy ISBN
ISBN 9780113311989 (Sold in a pack of 10 copies)

Printed in the United Kingdom for
The Stationery Office

N6116987   c2100   06/09

# Contents

# Acknowledgements

## AUTHORS

Simon Adams, Lloyds TSB
Alison Cartlidge, Steria
Ashley Hanna, HP
Stuart Rance, HP
John A Sowerby, DHL IT Services
John Windebank, Sun Microsystems

## REVIEWERS

Cassius Downs, Network Edge, USA
John Groom, West Groom Consulting, UK
Rosemary Gurney, Wardown Consulting, UK
Lou Hunnebeck, Third Sky, USA
Aidan Lawes, Service Management Evangelist, UK
Tricia Lewin, Independent Consultant, UK
Steve Mann, Opsys-sm2, UK
Michael McGaughey, Dream Catchers, USA
Trevor Murray, The Grey Matters, UK
Michael Imhoff Nielsen, IBM, Denmark
Christian Nissen, CFN People, Denmark
Sue Shaw, Tricentrica, UK

## EDITORS

Alison Cartlidge, Steria
Mark Lillycrop, itSMF UK

# About this guide

This guide provides a quick reference to the ITIL® framework for good practice in Service Management. It is designed as a study aid for students taking ITIL Foundation qualifications, and as a handy portable reference source for managers, practitioners, vendors and consultants, in the workplace and on the move.

This guide is not intended to replace the more detailed ITIL publications, nor to be a substitute for a course provider's training materials.

## USING THIS GUIDE TO OBTAIN THE ITIL FOUNDATION CERTIFICATE IN IT SERVICE MANAGEMENT

The content of this guide includes the learning experiences required by version 4.2 of the Foundation qualification syllabus. The guide also provides additional material for students and others who want a balanced level of understanding across the whole of ITIL. References to the ITIL core publications are provided with the relevant section headings.

To help students studying for the Foundation qualification, the headings in this guide are identified with one of the following symbols to indicate whether the knowledge they contain should be studied.

| Symbol | Significance |
|--------|--------------|
| ✔ | The syllabus requires knowledge of this topic. |
| ✔ | This is a key process or function which should be learned in more detail and for which there may be more questions in the exam. |
| ✘ | This is material that may be of interest to the reader but is not required for the exam. |

Specific terminology required by the syllabus is defined the first time it is used.

For more detail, see the current syllabus published by the APM Group.

Table 1 provides an alphabetical list of the ITIL Service Management processes with cross-references to the publication in which they are primarily defined, and where significant further expansion is provided. Most processes play a role during each lifecycle stage, but only significant references are included.

**Table 1  ITIL Service Management processes**

| Service Management process | Syllabus | Primary source | Further expansion |
|---|---|---|---|
| 7-Step Improvement Process | ✗ | CSI | |
| Access Management | ✓ | SO | |
| Availability Management | ✓ | SD | CSI |
| Capacity Management | ✓ | SD | SO, CSI |
| Change Management | ✓ | ST | |
| Demand Management | ✓ | SS | SD |
| Evaluation | ✗ | ST | |
| Event Management | ✓ | SO | |
| Financial Management | ✓ | SS | |
| Incident Management | ✓ | SO | CSI |
| Information Security Management | ✓ | SD | SO |
| IT Service Continuity Management | ✓ | SD | CSI |
| Knowledge Management | ✓ | ST | CSI |

| Problem Management | ✔ | SO | CSI |
|---|---|---|---|
| Release and Deployment Management | ✔ | ST | SO |
| Request Fulfilment | ✔ | SO | |
| Service Asset and Configuration Management | ✔ | ST | SO |
| Service Catalogue Management | ✔ | SD | SS |
| Service Level Management | ✔ | SD | CSI |
| Service Measurement | ✘ | CSI | |
| Service Portfolio Management | ✘ | SS | SD |
| Service Reporting | ✘ | CSI | |
| Service Validation and Testing | ✘ | ST | |
| Service Strategy (strategy generation) | ✘ | SS | |
| Supplier Management | ✔ | SD | |
| Transition Planning and Support | ✘ | ST | |
| **Function** | | | |
| Application Management | ✔ | SO | |
| IT Operations Management | ✔ | SO | |
| Service Desk | ✔ | SO | |
| Technical Management | ✔ | SO | |

*For the processes marked ✘, knowledge of some of their concepts is still required for Foundation. These are marked ✔ within the relevant chapters.*

*Note that the expansion of the acronyms can be found in section 1.2.*

# 1 Introduction to the ITIL Service Management framework

This quick-reference guide describes the key principles and practices of IT Service Management as a set of resources and capabilities such as processes, people and technology as described by the ITIL Service Management framework.

## 1.1 GOOD PRACTICE ✓

Organizations operating in dynamic environments need to improve their performance and maintain competitive advantage. Adopting good practices in industry-wide use can help to improve capability.

There are several sources for good practice:

- **Public frameworks and standards:** these have been validated across diverse environments; knowledge is widely distributed among professionals; there is publicly available training and certification; acquisition of knowledge through the labour market is easier
- **Proprietary knowledge of organizations and individuals:** this is customized for the local context and specific business needs; may only be available under commercial terms; may be tacit knowledge (inextricable and poorly documented).

## 1.2 THE ITIL FRAMEWORK ✓

The ITIL framework is a source of good practice in Service Management.

The ITIL library has the following components:

- **ITIL core:** best-practice publications applicable to all types of organizations that provide services to a business

■ **ITIL complementary guidance:** a complementary set of publications with guidance specific to industry sectors, organization types, operating models and technology architectures.

The objective of the ITIL Service Management framework is to provide services for customers that are fit for purpose, stable and so reliable that the business views them as a trusted provider. ITIL offers good-practice guidance applicable to all types of organizations that provide IT services to businesses. The framework is neither bureaucratic nor unwieldy if utilized sensibly and in full recognition of the business needs of the organization.

ITIL has been deployed successfully around the world for over 20 years. Over this time, the framework has evolved from a specialized set of Service Management topics with a focus on function, to a process-based framework which now provides a broader holistic Service Lifecycle.

**Definition: Service Lifecycle** ✔

The Service Lifecycle is an approach to IT Service Management that emphasizes the importance of coordination and control across the various functions, processes and systems necessary to manage the full lifecycle of IT services. The Service Management Lifecycle approach considers the strategy, design, transition, operation and continuous improvement of IT services.

The Service Lifecycle is described in a set of five publications within the ITIL core set. Each of these publications covers a stage of the Service Lifecycle (see Figure 1.1) from the initial definition and analysis of business requirements in *Service Strategy* (SS) and *Service Design* (SD), through migration into the live environment within *Service Transition* (ST), to live operation and improvement in *Service Operation* (SO) and *Continual Service Improvement* (CSI).

**Figure 1.1  The Service Lifecycle**

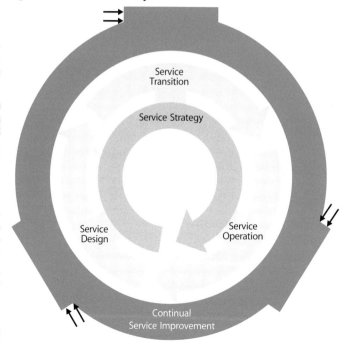

## 1.3    WHAT IS SERVICE MANAGEMENT?

To understand what Service Management is, we need to understand what services are, and how Service Management can help service providers to deliver and manage these services.

### Definition: Service ✔

A service is a means of delivering value to customers by facilitating outcomes that customers want to achieve without the ownership of specific costs and risks.

The outcomes that customers want to achieve are the reason why they purchase or use a service. The value of the service to the customer is directly dependent on how well a service facilitates these outcomes.

Service Management is what enables a service provider to understand the services they are providing; to ensure that the services really do facilitate the outcomes their customers want to achieve; to understand the value of the services to their customers; and to understand and manage all of the costs and risks associated with those services.

### Definition: Service Management ✔

Service Management is a set of specialized organizational capabilities for providing value to customers in the form of services.

These 'specialized organizational capabilities' are described in this guide. They include the processes, activities, functions and roles that a service provider uses to enable them to deliver services to their customers, as well as the ability to organize, manage knowledge, and understand how to facilitate outcomes that create value.

Service Management is concerned with more than just delivering services. Each service, process or infrastructure component has a lifecycle, and Service Management considers the entire lifecycle from strategy through design and transition to operation and continual improvement.

## 1.4 THE ITIL SERVICE MANAGEMENT MODEL

All services should be driven by business needs and requirements. Within this context they must also reflect the strategies and policies of the service provider organization, as indicated in Figure 1.2.

*Figure 1.2 Key links, inputs and outputs of the Service Lifecycle stages*

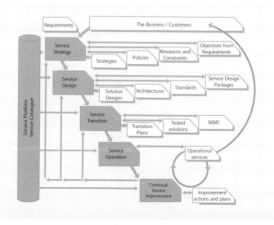

Figure 1.2 illustrates how the Service Lifecycle is initiated from a change in requirements in the business. These requirements are identified and agreed at the Service Strategy stage within a Service Level Package (SLP) and a defined set of business outcomes.

This passes to the Service Design stage where a service solution is produced together with a Service Design Package (SDP) containing everything necessary to take this service through the remaining stages of the lifecycle.

The SDP passes to the Service Transition stage, where the service is evaluated, tested and validated, and the service is transitioned into the live environment, where it enters the Service Operation stage.

Service Operation focuses on providing effective and efficient operational services to deliver the required business outcomes and value to the customer.

Continual Service Improvement identifies opportunities for improvement anywhere within any of the lifecycle stages, based on measurement and reporting of the efficiency, effectiveness, cost-effectiveness and compliance of services, Service Management processes and technology.

The ITIL lifecycle uses models to refine and customize an organization's use of the ITIL practices. These models are intended to be re-usable in a variety of organizational contexts and help to take advantage of economies of scale and efficiencies.

Central to these models are the overarching process elements that interact throughout the lifecycle.

Figure 1.3 shows the high-level basic flow of lifecycle process elements in the Service Management model.

**Figure 1.3  A high-level view of the ITIL Service Management model**

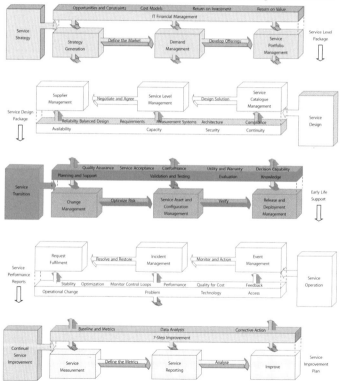

Figure 1.4 provides a pictorial representation of the key processes defined by each publication and lifecycle stage.

*Figure 1.4  ITIL v3 Service Management processes across the Service Lifecycle*

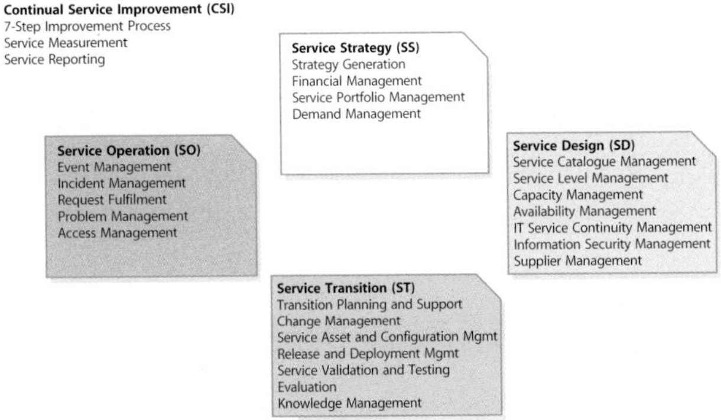

**Continual Service Improvement (CSI)**
7-Step Improvement Process
Service Measurement
Service Reporting

**Service Strategy (SS)**
Strategy Generation
Financial Management
Service Portfolio Management
Demand Management

**Service Operation (SO)**
Event Management
Incident Management
Request Fulfilment
Problem Management
Access Management

**Service Design (SD)**
Service Catalogue Management
Service Level Management
Capacity Management
Availability Management
IT Service Continuity Management
Information Security Management
Supplier Management

**Service Transition (ST)**
Transition Planning and Support
Change Management
Service Asset and Configuration Mgmt
Release and Deployment Mgmt
Service Validation and Testing
Evaluation
Knowledge Management

# 2    Service Strategy

Service Strategy establishes an overall strategy for IT services and for IT Service Management.

## 2.1    GOALS, OBJECTIVES, SCOPE AND VALUE (SS 1.3)

### 2.1.1    Goals  ✔

The *Service Strategy* publication helps IT service providers review and develop their abilities to:

■ Operate and grow successfully in the long term
■ Think and act in a strategic manner
■ Transform their Service Management capabilities into a strategic asset
■ See and act on the relationships between the IT services, processes and systems, and the business objectives that they support
■ Handle the costs and risks associated with their Service Portfolios.

### 2.1.2    Objectives  ✔

When an IT organization adopts a clear Service Strategy that reflects the strategies and policies of the service provider's overall organization, all IT service solutions and activities can be driven by identified business needs and requirements.

The objectives of a robust Service Strategy need to address the following concepts:

### 2.1.2.1  Delivering customer 'outcomes'

To be successful, the Service Strategy of any service provider must direct the development and provision of services that are perceived by the customer as delivering real value to them, in the form of outcomes that the customer needs to achieve.

### 2.1.2.2  Understanding the market place

To achieve a deep understanding of customer requirements (in terms of what their needs are and when and why they occur), the service provider must first make sure that they have a clear understanding of who their existing or potential future customers are. This requires the service provider to understand the wider context of the current and potential market places that the service provider does, or could, operate in.

### 2.1.2.3  Serving the stakeholders

A successful Service Strategy cannot be created in isolation from the over-arching strategy and culture of the organization that the service provider belongs to. The service provider may exist within an organization solely to deliver service to one specific business unit, to service multiple business units, or to operate as an external service provider serving multiple external businesses. The strategy they adopt must provide sufficient value to their customers and all the service provider's other stakeholders – it must fulfil the service provider's strategic purpose.

### 2.1.2.4  Acknowledging competition and choice

The Service Strategy of all service providers must recognize the existence of competition, and embody an awareness that customers and suppliers always have choices, irrespective of the context in which they operate. Therefore, a Service Strategy must describe how that service provider will be differentiated from the competition. All service providers have customers. All service providers have current or potential competition. All need a Service Strategy.

### 2.1.3   Scope   ✗

The guidance in the *Service Strategy* volume is relevant across all aspects of the Service Lifecycle and includes:

- Formation and implementation of strategy
- Development of markets and offerings
- Service assets and value creation
- Service Portfolio Management and Service Catalogue
- Financial Management
- Demand Management
- Organizational development and culture
- Sourcing strategy
- Strategic risks.

### 2.1.4   Value to business   ✗

Any investment in Service Strategy must deliver business value in return. These benefits typically encompass:

- Improved use of IT investments
- Tight coupling between the perception of business and IT value
- Performance and measures that are business value based
- Service development investment decisions driven by business priorities and clear Return on Investment (ROI) plans
- Agile adaptation of IT services to pre-empt and meet changing business needs
- Clear visibility of linkages between business services and IT service assets.

## 2.2    KEY PRINCIPLES

### 2.2.1    Service assets–the basis for value creation (SS 3.2.1) ✔

*Figure 2.1  Service delivery through service assets*

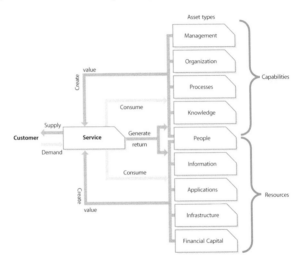

Figure 2.1 demonstrates how IT service providers utilize their assets in the form of resources and capabilities to create each service that they provide.

### Definition: Resources ✔

This is a generic term that includes IT infrastructure, people, money or anything else that might help to deliver an IT service. Resources are considered to be assets of an organization.

### Definition: Capabilities ✔

The ability of an organization, person, process, application, Configuration Item or IT service to carry out an activity. Capabilities are intangible assets of an organization.

### Definition: Assets ✔

Assets can be any resource or capability. Assets can be one of the following types: management, organization, process, knowledge, people, information, applications, infrastructure or financial capital.

### Definition: Service asset ✔

A service asset is the resource or capability of a service provider. Service assets include anything that could contribute to the delivery of a service.

The key difference between resource assets and capability assets is that, typically, distinctive capabilities can only be developed over time. Capabilities reflect experience and are used to transform resources into services.

The distinctive capabilities of a service provider set it apart from its competitors, and enable it to attract and retain customers by offering unique value propositions.

## 2.2.2   Value creation through services (SS 3.1.1, 3.1.2) ✗

An IT service provider has a set of assets in the form of capabilities and resources that it uses to create IT services for its customers. Each of its customers also has its own assets (resources and capabilities) and uses IT services to enable those customer assets to generate business value.

A customer of the IT service provider only perceives value from the IT services it receives if a direct connection can be made between the IT service and the business value it needs to generate. Therefore, it is essential that IT service providers focus on understanding, articulating and measuring how effective their services are in enabling their customers to achieve their desired outcomes. It is also important that the IT service provider acknowledges that there is frequently a difference between what the customer perceives as valuable and what the IT organization believes it provides. Understanding the outcomes that are important to the customer is critical to the success of the IT service provider.

## 2.2.3   Value in the form of utility and warranty (SS 2.2.2, 3.1.3) ✔

Customers value an IT service when they see a clear relationship between that IT service and the business value they need to generate. The degree of value each customer perceives from an IT service is made up of two components: Service Utility and Service Warranty.

## Definition: Service Utility ✔

Service Utility is the functionality of an IT service from the customer's perspective. The business value of an IT service is created by the combination of the Service Utility (what the service does) and Service Warranty (how well it does it).

## Definition: Service Warranty ✔

Service Warranty is the assurance that an IT service will meet agreed requirements. This may be a formal agreement such as a Service Level Agreement (SLA) or contract, or may be a marketing message or brand image. The business value of an IT service is created by the combination of the Service Utility (what the service does) and Service Warranty (how well it does it).

Utility and Warranty are not optional components. Both must exist for an IT service to provide value to the customer. Service Utility defines the purpose of a service, while Service Warranty defines the required performance of the service in terms of Capacity, Availability, Continuity and Security.

### 2.2.4   Business Case (SS 5.2.1) ✔

## Definition: Business Case ✔

The Business Case is the justification for a significant item of expenditure. It includes information about costs, benefits, options, issues, risks and possible problems.

A service provider will need to make decisions on what Service Management initiatives it wishes to invest in. The Business Case for these investments is key to this decision-making process.

A Business Case is a decision support and planning tool. It describes the objectives and the likely outcomes of a business decision.

The Business Case articulates the objectives of the initiative and the specific business impacts (costs, risks and benefits) that the initiative is expected to generate. The financial consequence of a decision, typically in the form of Return on Investment (ROI), is often a core component of a Business Case.

A well-rounded Business Case also covers an analysis of the desired non-financial business impacts associated with the initiative, forming clear linkages between these non-financial impacts and a recognized business objective. This analysis may use the Value of Investment (VOI) technique described in Continual Service Improvement.

The structure of a Business Case generally covers:

- Introduction
- Methods and assumptions
- Business impacts
- Risks and contingencies
- Recommendations.

## 2.2.5  Service Model (SS 7.2.1)  ✗

A Service Model is a diagram that represents a service. It helps to show how the service provider creates value, by linking the service assets to customer requirements.

A Service Model describes the structure and the dynamics of the service:

- **Structure:** the particular service assets needed to deliver the service and the patterns in which they are configured. A typical structure will show servers, networks and other hardware and software components, with the connectivity between them. This model will often be used by technical management to help design, test and support infrastructure
- **Dynamics:** the activities, flow of resources, coordination and interactions between customer and service provider assets. A typical dynamic structure will show timings, triggers and events. This model will often be used by Application Management to help design, test and support applications and end-to-end services.

A Service Model may include:

- Process maps
- Workflow diagrams
- Queuing models
- Activity patterns.

## 2.2.6  Characteristics of a process (SS 2.6.2, SD 2.3.2) ✔

### Definition: Process ✔

A process is a structured set of activities designed to accomplish a specific objective. It takes one or more defined inputs and turns them into defined outputs. A process may include any of the roles, responsibilities, tools and management controls required to reliably deliver the outputs. A process may define policies, standards, guidelines, activities and work instructions if they are needed.

Processes have the following characteristics. They

- Are **defined** in terms of actions, dependencies and sequence
- Are **measurable**, in management terms such as cost and quality, and in practitioner terms such as duration and productivity
- Exist to deliver **specific results** that are identifiable and countable
- Have **customers** or **stakeholders** with expectations that must be met by the results that the process delivers
- Respond to **specific events** which act as triggers for the process.

## 2.3    PROCESSES AND ACTIVITIES

Chapter 4 of the *Service Strategy* publication describes a number of activities which are called the Service Strategy process in the Foundation syllabus, and the strategy generation process in the *Introduction to the ITIL Service Lifecycle*. These activities are:

- Define the market
- Develop the offerings
- Develop strategic assets
- Prepare for execution.

### 2.3.1    Define the market (SS 4.1)  ✗

#### 2.3.1.1    Objectives ✗, scope ✗ and value ✗

Achieving a deep understanding of customer needs, in terms of what those needs are, and when and why they occur, also requires a clear understanding of who is an existing or potential customer of that service provider. This, in turn, requires the service provider to understand the wider context of the current and potential market places that the service provider operates in or may wish to operate in.

### 2.3.1.2    Basic concepts ✗

When embarking upon an exercise to define the markets within which a service provider needs to operate, it is important to take stock of what the aim of this exercise is; i.e. what is the purpose of the strategy being considered?

When this is understood it is possible to gain a clear understanding of the customers that need to be served, leading to identification of the opportunities that these customers present to the service provider. From this exercise the service provider can classify and visualize how the services they provide interact with their portfolio of customers to generate business value.

### 2.3.1.3    Activities ✗

Understanding the purpose of the strategy

There are two distinct perspectives to the creation of Service Strategy:

- **Services for Strategies:** a Service Strategy may be required to identify and develop the services that are required to enable an organization to achieve its overall business strategy
- **Strategies for Services:** a service provider should develop a Service Strategy for the services it offers, which differentiates its services from those offered by its competition.

Understanding the customer

A service provider can only achieve a real understanding of the customers they serve once they have consciously considered and identified who their customers are, and who their target customers need to be to fulfil the needs of their Service Strategy. This requires the service provider to take time out to consider their current and planned operating models to achieve a clear understanding of the type of service provider they are or what they may need to become one.

**Service provider types** ✔ are classified as:

- **Type I:** exists within an organization solely to deliver service to one specific business unit
- **Type II:** services multiple business units in the same organization
- **Type III:** operates as an external service provider serving multiple external customers.

As discussed in section 2.2.1, each customer of the IT service provider has its own assets. Business managers within the customer organization make investment decisions regarding which assets they need to develop in-house and what external services are needed to supplement and enhance these internal assets to enable their desired business outcomes to be achieved.

IT service providers must strive to understand their customers, and understand the outcomes that their customers are trying to achieve through use of the IT services provided.

It is only when the service provider understands the reason for their customer wanting their services that the provider can truly understand the value that the customer perceives they receive from use of those services.

## Understanding the opportunity

By gaining deep insight into the outcomes that each target customer is trying to achieve, the service provider can identify opportunities. Service opportunities exist wherever there are customer outcomes that are not well supported by the existing service market place.

This insight into the customer's business strategies and how well their desired outcomes are being supported is achieved through the role of customer focused Business Relationship Managers (BRMs).

### Classifying and visualizing

It is likely that each customer of an IT service provider will take a unique combination of the services in that provider's portfolio. It is also likely that each customer will use these IT services in a way that is unique to their assets and the business outcomes they are striving to achieve.

It is useful for IT service providers to visualize their services in terms of a service archetype (e.g. design, support, monitor, secure) and the type of customer asset supported (e.g. processes, infrastructure, applications). This can help lead to a better understanding of how customers combine the IT services with their own assets to achieve business outcomes. It can also help to show overlaps and connections between different services.

## 2.3.2   Develop the offerings (SS 4.2)   ✘

### 2.3.2.1   Objectives ✘, scope ✘ and value ✘

When a service provider understands the markets that they need to serve, they are in a position to develop the service offerings to enable the service provider to thrive in those markets.

To develop the appropriate portfolio of service offerings the service provider must consider the discrete market spaces in which they will operate, and be able to articulate their services in terms of the specific outcomes the service needs to facilitate for each target customer.

### 2.3.2.2   Activities ✗

Market space

Sets of business outcomes, which can be facilitated by a service, define one or more market spaces.

For example, a secure online payment service enables retailers to offer their shoppers more options of how to buy from the supplier, which attracts more customers to that supplier and generates more transactions. This is a desired business outcome, facilitated by an IT service.

Outcome-based definition of services

Each market space represents a set of opportunities for a service provider to deliver value to customers through one or more of its services. However, each market space may use the service provider's services in different ways, achieving different business outcomes. This can lead to issues when services are described in Service Level Agreements simply in terms of resources made available to customers without reference to the context in which that service is likely to be used in that market space.

An outcome-based definition of a service enables the service provider to consider and deliver that service from the perspective of the market space in which it will be used to generate desired business outcomes.

Well-formed service definitions, that are market-space specific, facilitate effective and efficient Service Management by the service provider.

Service Portfolio, Pipeline and Catalogue

Establishing a clear understanding of a service provider's Service Portfolio is critical to that service provider's success in developing the right offerings. The concepts of Service Portfolio, Pipeline and Catalogue are discussed under Service Portfolio Management in section 2.3.5.

## 2.3.3   Develop strategic assets (SS 4.3)  ✗

### 2.3.3.1   Objectives ✗, scope ✗ and value ✗

A service provider's success is largely dependent upon their ability to become distinctive in the market spaces they serve. Service Management can be used as a strategic asset to achieve this distinctiveness by increasing the value of each service to the customer, which in turn generates greater service demand.

### 2.3.3.2   Activities ✗

Service Management as a strategic asset

Service providers should regard an effective and mature Service Management capability as the basis for their core competency, distinctive performance and long-lasting advantage in their market space. From this perspective, the service provider's Service Management capability becomes a strategic asset to them.

Furthermore, when a service provider achieves a proven ability to consistently deliver trusted services to a customer, which the customer regards as highly valuable to them, the customer perceives those services from the service provider as its own strategic asset. Sourcing services from that service provider enables the customer to achieve distinct performance in its own specific market space.

## Service Management as a closed-loop control system

*Figure 2.2  Service Management as a closed-loop control system*

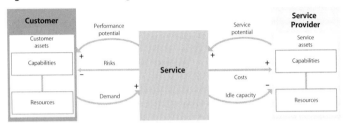

Figure 2.2 demonstrates that the service provider's service assets are the source of value, and the customer's service assets are the recipients. Value is delivered to the customer by increasing the performance potential of the customer's assets and reducing the customer's risks. This in turn creates a demand for this service.

### Definition: Risk ✔

Risk is a possible event that could cause harm or loss, or affect the ability to achieve objectives. It is measured by the probability of a threat, the vulnerability of the asset to that threat, and the impact it would have if it occurred.

Risk can also be defined as uncertainty of outcome, whether positive opportunity or negative threat.

Service improvement initiatives by the service provider act to increase the efficiency and effectiveness of its service assets, which increases the service potential of these assets. This increases the value of that service to the customer by increasing the potential performance gains the customer can achieve from its own assets and/or further reducing the customer's risks. This further increases demand upon that service provider for that service, and therefore reduces the idle (unused) service capacity that remains within the service provider.

### 2.3.4  Prepare for execution (SS 4.4)  ✗

#### 2.3.4.1  Objectives ✗, scope ✗ and value ✗

Strategy is critical to the long-term survival and success of every service provider. Forming an effective Service Strategy that is relevant to a specific service provider requires sufficient investment in preparation. This is time taken out of the day-to-day operational business cycle to reflect, examine, formulate options and prioritize the selected strategic options.

#### 2.3.4.2  Activities ✗

Figure 2.3 describes the key steps involved in forming an effective Service Strategy.

## Figure 2.3 Service Strategy formulation

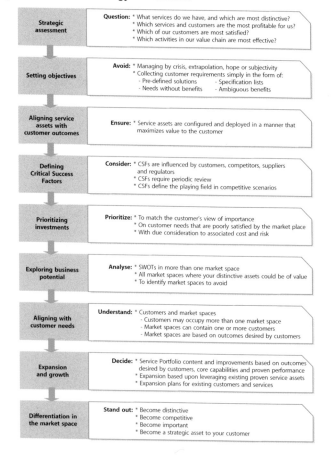

| Strategic assessment | **Question:** * What services do we have, and which are most distinctive?<br>* Which services and customers are the most profitable for us?<br>* Which of our customers are most satisfied?<br>* Which activities in our value chain are most effective? |
|---|---|
| Setting objectives | **Avoid:** * Managing by crisis, extrapolation, hope or subjectivity<br>* Collecting customer requirements simply in the form of:<br>  - Pre-defined solutions    - Specification lists<br>  - Needs without benefits  - Ambiguous benefits |
| Aligning service assets with customer outcomes | **Ensure:** * Service assets are configured and deployed in a manner that maximizes value to the customer |
| Defining Critical Success Factors | **Consider:** * CSFs are influenced by customers, competitors, suppliers and regulators<br>* CSFs require periodic review<br>* CSFs define the playing field in competitive scenarios |
| Prioritizing investments | **Prioritize:** * To match the customer's view of importance<br>* On customer needs that are poorly satisfied by the market place<br>* With due consideration to associated cost and risk |
| Exploring business potential | **Analyse:** * SWOTs in more than one market space<br>* All market spaces where your distinctive assets could be of value<br>* To identify market spaces to avoid |
| Aligning with customer needs | **Understand:** * Customers and market spaces<br>  - Customers may occupy more than one market space<br>  - Market spaces can contain one or more customers<br>  - Market spaces are based on outcomes desired by customers |
| Expansion and growth | **Decide:** * Service Portfolio content and improvements based on outcomes desired by customers, core capabilities and proven performance<br>* Expansion based upon leveraging existing proven service assets<br>* Expansion plans for existing customers and services |
| Differentiation in the market space | **Stand out:** * Become distinctive<br>* Become competitive<br>* Become important<br>* Become a strategic asset to your customer |

### 2.3.5  Service Portfolio Management (SS 5.3, 5.4, B2.1)  ✗

Whilst knowledge of the Service Portfolio Management (SPM) process is not required for the ITIL Foundation exam, some specific concepts are required and these are indicated with a ✔.

#### 2.3.5.1   Objectives ✗, scope ✗ and value ✗

Service Portfolio Management is the process by which a service provider proactively manages its investments across the Service Lifecycle, considering each service in terms of the business value it provides.

Service Portfolio Management enables:

- Each customer to understand:
    - What services are available
    - What charges are associated with each service
    - Why they should use these services
    - Why they should take these services from that specific service provider

- The service provider to understand:
    - What strengths, weaknesses and gaps exist in their Service Portfolio
    - What their investment priorities and risks are
    - How their service assets (resources and capabilities) should be allocated to address these priorities and risks.

### 2.3.5.2    Basic concepts  ✗

A Service Portfolio describes each service in terms of business value, the business needs addressed and how the service provider responds to those needs.

> **Definition: Service Portfolio**  ✔
>
> The Service Portfolio is the complete set of services that are managed by a service provider. It is used to manage the entire lifecycle of all services, and includes three categories: Service Pipeline (proposed or in development); Service Catalogue (live or available for deployment); and Retired Services.

**Figure 2.4  The Service Portfolio, Pipeline and Catalogue**

### 2.3.5.3    Activities  ✗

Key activities for Service Portfolio Management are:

- **Define:** collection of a validated inventory of all existing and proposed services including their business cases
- **Analyse:** identification of what services are required to enable the organization to achieve its service goals, how well the existing Service Portfolio meets these needs, what service assets are required to enable the Service Strategy and how to align and prioritize to meet demand

- **Approve:** finalization of the desired future state of the Service Portfolio and authorization of retention of appropriate existing services, and required investment in the replacement, rationalization, refactoring, renewal or retirement of existing services
- **Charter:** communication of approved decisions relating to desired changes to the Service Portfolio and the execution of actions to promote newly chartered services into Service Design; refresh selected existing services in the Service Catalogue; and initiate Service Transition activities.

### 2.3.5.4  Roles ✗

Each set of related services in the Service Portfolio is owned by a Product Manager. This role is also referred to as a Service Manager.

Product Manager responsibilities include:

- Managing services as a product over their entire lifecycle from concept to retirement, through design, transition and operation
- Instrumental in developing the Service Strategy and executing the strategy through the Service Lifecycle.

### 2.3.6  Demand Management (SS 5.5) ✔

### 2.3.6.1  Objectives ✔, scope ✗ and value ✗

Services cannot be produced in advance of when they are consumed; therefore it is essential that the service provider achieves a tight synchronization of supply capacity and service demand.

Both the service provider and its customers benefit from the efficiency and consistency in service quality that this brings.

### 2.3.6.2   Basic concepts ✔

Demand Management is used by service providers to achieve the most effective utilization of their service assets by understanding and influencing how and when demand arrives from their customers.

Demand Management is the process by which a service provider gathers a clear understanding of the Patterns of Business Activity (PBA) of each of its customers that generate demand, and seeks to influence how and when these demand patterns are formed.

#### Patterns of Business Activity

Customer PBAs influence what the service provider sees in the form of patterns of demand for its services. Therefore, it is important that service providers study the business of each of their customers to identify, analyse and codify these patterns. PBAs are generated by customer assets such as people, processes and applications.

#### User profile

The user profile (UP) defines a pattern of user demand for IT services. Each user profile includes one or more PBA. For example, particular roles in a customer organization, such as 'senior executive' or 'highly mobile sales executive', may have an associated user profile. User profiles may also relate to specific business processes or applications, such as a payment processing system or a customer assistance process. Demand Management helps to define differentiated services and service packages that will meet the needs of the customers.

### 2.3.6.3   Activities ✔

#### Activity-based Demand Management

This is the technique by which a service provider studies a customer's business to understand the PBAs which generate demand for service. This provides essential information to Capacity Management.

Analysing and tracking the activity patterns of the business process enables prediction of demand for the IT services that support the process. This in turn enables prediction of demand for the underlying service assets that support those services. Activity-based Demand Management can consolidate demand patterns to ensure that the business plans of customers are synchronized with Service Management plans, such as the Capacity Plan.

Where appropriate, PBAs can be associated with specific types of users and the activities of each customer. This analysis builds user profiles that codify the nature and timing of the demand for services, allowing the customer and the service provider to understand how, when and from whom service demand will be generated.

### 2.3.6.4 Challenges ✓

- Unmanaged, and therefore uncertain, demand for services is a significant source of risk to the service provider
- Insufficient capacity has impact on the quality of services delivered and limits the growth of the service
- Excess capacity generates cost without creating the value that provides a basis for cost recovery. Sometimes an amount of unused capacity is necessary to deliver service levels and thus ensure a higher level of assurance
- The delivery schedule that the service provider has planned for dictates the available service capacity, largely irrespective of the actual level of demand. Unless the Capacity Plan is driven by a clear understanding of the customer's PBA, it is highly likely that the service provider will be faced with periods of unused capacity (waste) and unserved demand (lost opportunity and customer dissatisfaction).

### 2.3.6.5   Key metrics ✗

- ■ Business activities to support definition of PBAs and ongoing monitoring/maintenance
- ■ Actual demand patterns to support activity/demand modelling.

### 2.3.6.6   Roles ✗

The Business Relationship Managers are a key interface to understanding PBAs and influencing customer demand.

### 2.3.7   Financial Management (SS 5.1) ✓

### 2.3.7.1   Objectives ✓, scope ✗ and value ✗

Financial Management quantifies, in clear financial terms, the value of IT services and the underpinning service assets. It helps service providers to understand and control the factors that influence supply and demand and to deliver services as cost-effectively as possible.

The Financial Management data used by an IT organization may reside in, and be owned by, the accounting and finance domain, but responsibility for generating and utilizing it extends to other areas. Financial Management aggregates data inputs from across the enterprise and assists in generating and disseminating information as an output to feed critical decisions and activities.

Financial Management is applicable to all three service provider types.

IT service providers use Financial Management to support the development and execution of their Service Strategy, achieving:

- ■ Enhanced decision making
- ■ Speed of change

- Service Portfolio Management
- Financial compliance and control
- Operational control
- Value capture and creation.

Financial Management provides guiding information for a Continual Service Improvement Strategy, to ensure service improvement investment decisions are based upon sound financial considerations of the balance between the cost of an improvement and the additional value that it will provide to the customer in terms of desired business outcomes.

### 2.3.7.2    Basic concepts ✔

Service valuation

Service valuation is used within Financial Management to identify:

- **Provisioning value:** the cost to the IT service provider of delivering a specific service to a customer. This includes costs associated with hardware and software, annual maintenance fees, personnel, facilities and power consumption, compliance, taxes and interest charges
- **Service value potential:** techniques such as service-oriented accounting are used to associate specific monetary values with each perceived value-added component of the service. The sum of these perceived values is the service value potential, which is added to the provisioning value to calculate the ultimate value of the service.

Demand modelling

Financial demand modelling focuses on identifying the total cost of service utilization to the customer, and predicting the financial implications of future service demand.

Return on Investment

Return on Investment (ROI) quantifies the value of an investment and, in Service Management, is used as a measure of the ability to use assets to generate additional value.

### 2.3.7.3    Activities  ✗

Service-oriented accounting

This is used to achieve an understanding of services in terms of consumption and provisioning, and enable appropriate translation between corporate financial systems and Service Management.

The Financial Management data used by service providers may be owned by the accounting and financial departments, but all departments need to understand their individual obligations to generate and utilize the data collated and disseminated by Financial Management.

Accounting

Financial Management addresses the relationship between corporate financial systems and Service Management. It enables services to be provisioned as cost-effectively as possible and the cost structures to be visible.

Ongoing analysis of the cost structure of each service provides the operational financial information that the service provider needs to continually tune each service to achieve the most appropriate balance between the cost of service provision and the value that each service can offer to the customer.

### 2.3.7.4    Challenges  ✗
- Monitoring tools providing utilization information are inaccurate or too costly

- Lack of planning information, within service provider and customers.

### 2.3.7.5    Key metrics  ✗
- Service utilization data, including by service, customers, users, department etc.
- Financial trends for funding, value and accounting.

### 2.3.7.6    Roles  ✗
Some organizations have dedicated IT Finance Managers, whilst others may share the activities amongst the senior IT managers, especially those with responsibilities for other key Service Management processes, e.g. Service Level Manager. Key responsibilities include:

- Budgeting and forecasting, with charging, where relevant
- Accounting, including developing policies, cost models and supporting cost-benefit cases for investment
- Support internal/external auditors.

# 3   Service Design

The Service Design stage takes business requirements and creates services, their supporting practices and management tools which meet business demands for quality, reliability and flexibility.

## 3.1   GOALS, OBJECTIVES, SCOPE AND VALUE (SD 2.4, 3.1)

### 3.1.1   Goals ✔

Key goals for Service Design are to:

- Drive consistency in the design of new or significantly changed services
- Consider the impact on the overall service, the management systems and tools, technology architectures, processes and measurement methods, and metrics
- Ensure that all management and operational requirements are recognized and addressed as a fundamental part of the design activities, reducing the likelihood of issues arising in later stages of the Service Lifecycle.

### 3.1.2   Objectives ✔

Service Design focuses on linking business outcomes, objectives and their underpinning processes and functions directly to the IT services and their underlying assets, processes and functions.

The main objectives are to:

- Design services to satisfy business objectives which can easily and efficiently be maintained and enhanced
- Design efficient and effective processes for high-quality IT services

- Identify and manage risks – remove or mitigate them
- Design secure and resilient technologies, resources and capability
- Design measurement methods and metrics for assessing effectiveness and efficiency and to support service improvement.

### 3.1.3   Scope  ✗

There are five aspects to Service Design, covering the design of:

- New or changed services
- Service Management systems and tools
- Technology architecture and management systems
- The processes required
- Measurement methods and metrics.

These five aspects of design are covered more fully in sections 3.2.3 and 3.3.1.4.

Requirements are extracted from the Service Portfolio, analysed, documented and agreed and then used as the basis for the design of the new or changed service, as illustrated in Figure 3.1.

Not every change in an IT service requires Service Design activity; it will only be required for 'significant' changes. However, 'significant' needs to be defined to ensure clarity on when Service Design is required.

## Figure 3.1  Aligning new services to business requirements

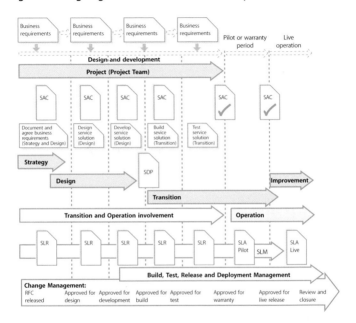

### 3.1.4   Value to business ✔

The following benefits result from good Service Design:

■  Improved consistency across all services and better
integration with infrastructure components, leading to faster
and simpler implementation, and improved quality of service

■  Clear alignment with business needs demonstrated through
a focus on IT measurements directly related to key aspects of
business performance

■ More effective and relevant processes, with improved measurement methods and metrics, enabling informed decision making.

## 3.2    KEY PRINCIPLES

### 3.2.1    The four Ps of Service Design (SD 2.4.2) ✔

It is key to recognize the importance of the 'four Ps' to successful service provision:

■ People
■ Processes
■ Products
■ Partners.

When designing new or changed service, Service Design focuses on ensuring the 'four Ps' are taken into account at every stage throughout the Service Lifecycle. This is achieved through the five major design aspects.

### 3.2.2    Balance in Service Design (SD 3.2) ✘

At its heart Service Design involves a delicate balancing act. Initially this is between the functionality requirements and the performance requirements, Service Utility and Service Warranty. Service Design must understand and evaluate the implications for the resulting business value of the service in finding the balance.

Next the realities of resource availability must be considered. What technology, people and skills will be required? How much budget is available to move through the Service Lifecycle from transition into operation? What are the forecast business-as-usual costs for running the service?

Finally the constraints of the timescale available to move the service into operation must be taken into account.

Good Service Design must balance all of the above to ensure an effective end result.

### 3.2.3   The five design aspects (SD 2.4.2)   ✔

Service Design takes into consideration five major aspects of service provision for which the design activities must be carried out.

- **Service solutions:** including all of the functional requirements, resources and capabilities needed and agreed
- **Service Management systems and tools** (especially the Service Portfolio): to ensure consistency with other services and guarantee that supporting and dependent services are adequate to maintain ongoing reliable service delivery
- **Technology architectures and management systems:** to ensure they are consistent with the new service and are suitable to operate and maintain it
- **Processes:** to ensure the process, roles and responsibilities are adequate to operate, support and maintain the new or changed service
- **Measurement methods and metrics:** to ensure the methods can provide the required metrics on the service.

See section 3.3.1.4 for further detail on the five aspects of design.

However, these design activities must not happen in isolation. As requirements are turned into a design, the implications for each of the other four design aspects must also be taken into account.

### 3.2.4   Service Design Package (SD Appendix A)  ✔

#### Definition: Service Design Package  ✔

A Service Design Package (SDP) is the document(s) defining all aspects of an IT service and its requirements through each stage of its lifecycle. An SDP is produced for each new IT service, major change, or IT service retirement.

The Service Design Package is the significant product of the Service Design stage. It is assembled using the output from the various processes, methods and techniques employed throughout Service Design, and is the foundation document supporting the subsequent transition, operation and continual improvement of the new or changed service.

At a high level the SDP includes the following:

- Requirements
- Service design
- Organizational Readiness Assessment
- Service Lifecycle plans including programme, transition and operational acceptance plans
- Service Acceptance Criteria (SAC).

### 3.2.5   Delivery model options (SD 3.11)  ✘

As part of the Service Design, and a major input to the SDP, an Organizational Readiness Assessment is carried out. This assesses the current capability of the organization against the requirements of the new or changed service.

A number of service-sourcing strategies are available to fill any gaps identified.

- **Insourcing:** using internal resources
- **Outsourcing:** using the resources of an external organization
- **Co-sourcing:** a number of organizations working together to provide key parts of the solution
- **Partnership or multi-sourcing:** formal arrangements between two or more organizations to work together in a strategic partnership to deliver a service, sharing the rewards
- **Business Process Outsourcing (BPO):** one organization takes over the provision of an entire business function on behalf of another – e.g. payroll and call centre operations
- **Application service provision:** an application service provider (ASP) allows access to shared computer-based services to another – sometimes called 'on-demand services'
- **Knowledge Process Outsourcing (KPO):** one organization provides domain-based, specialized services for another. Differs from BPO in that it offers the opportunity to avoid the need to develop specialist knowledge or experience in-house – e.g. credit rating or benchmarking.

Each of these sourcing options comes with its own pros and cons which need to be considered, along with the potential for added complexity and increased risk, when deciding on an appropriate delivery model as part of the Service Design.

## 3.3     PROCESSES AND ACTIVITIES

### 3.3.1   Designing services   ✗

Whilst knowledge of the designing services activity is not required for the ITIL Foundation exam, some specific concepts are required and these are indicated with a ✔.

### 3.3.1.1    Identifying service requirements (SD 3.3)   ✗

Service requirements are a formal statement of what is needed
– for example, a Service Level Requirement, a Project
Requirement or the required deliverables for a process.

Service Design must consider all elements of the service to ensure
that the end-result meets the Service Utility and Warranty
requirements of the customer. These include:

- Business process that the service is intended to support
- Scalability requirements to ensure the service will continue to
  meet current and future demand
- Legal or regulatory compliance requirements, e.g. required
  security levels
- Required measurements and metrics
- The service itself and its SLA
- The supporting services delivered either by internal providers
  and covered by an Operational Level Agreement (OLA), or by
  external suppliers covered by an underpinning contract
- The technology required to support and deliver the service:
  the data, applications, infrastructure and environment.

Often the delivery of services is increasingly complex, involving
many internal and external suppliers in the end-to-end delivery.
In such cases a Service Design Authority should be established to
ensure consistency and integrity across all components of the
service.

Changes in the requirements relating to any of the aspects must
be considered in the context of all of the other aspects to ensure
potential impacts are understood and properly taken into
account.

### 3.3.1.2    Identifying business requirements and drivers (SD 3.4)    ✗

IT must maintain accurate information on business requirements and drivers to enable it to ensure that the services it provides continue to provide business value. This includes requirements for new services and also covers new or changed requirements for existing services. Time spent on this activity early in the Service Design will avoid problems with customer satisfaction and spiralling costs later.

The requirements need to be fully documented, agreed and signed off by senior responsible business owners. Changes in the requirements must be managed according to an approved process.

### 3.3.1.3    Design activities    ✗

The design process activities are:

- Requirements analysis
- Design of appropriate services
- Revision of processes and documents
- Liaison with other planning and design functions
- Risk assessment of design processes and deliverables
- Ensuring alignment with strategies and policies.

The main inputs to Service Design activities are:

- Corporate and business visions, strategies, policies and plans
- Legislative and regulatory constraints and requirements
- IT strategy, policies and plans
- Business requirements
- Service Portfolio
- Measurement tools and techniques.

The main outputs from the design activities are:

- Suggested revisions to strategies, policies and plans
- Revised designs, plans and technology and management architectures
- Designs for new or changed services, processes and technologies.

### 3.3.1.4    The five design aspects ✔

Designing service solutions (SD 3.6.1) ✔

A formal and structured approach is required to ensure a service with the right balance of functionality and cost, with agreed timescales. The process must be interactive and incremental – flexible enough to recognize and adopt changes in business requirements identified during the course of the design.

The areas to be considered include:

- Analyse the business requirements
- Explore opportunities for re-use
- Produce service solution designs
- Create and maintain the Service Acceptance Criteria (SAC)
- Evaluate and cost alternative designs
- Agree the expenditure and budgets
- Re-evaluate and confirm the business benefits
- Agree the preferred solution and its Service Level Requirements (SLRs)
- Ensure the solution is in line with strategies, policies, architecture and make proposals for change if not
- Ensure corporate and IT governance and security controls are taken into account
- Complete an Organizational Readiness Assessment
- Identify requirements for suppliers and supporting contracts
- Assemble the Service Design Package (SDP).

### Designing supporting systems (SD 3.6.2)  ✔

The most effective way of managing all aspects of services through their lifecycle is by using appropriate management systems and tools.

It is important that the design and development of these systems and tools is undertaken in the same way as for any other IT service to ensure it meets the needs of all stakeholders.

The Service Portfolio is the most critical management system used to support all processes, and describes a provider's services in terms of business value. It contains details of all services within the Service Pipeline, the Service Catalogue or the Retired Services Catalogue, dependent on the current stage of a service in the Service Lifecycle.

The Service Pipeline is used mainly in the Strategy and Design stages of the Service Lifecycle. It contains details of all new and changed business requirements that have not yet become services. It is not usually visible to the customer or support teams.

The Service Catalogue is managed in Service Design through the Service Catalogue Management process and is used through the design, transition and operation stages of the Service Lifecycle. It is visible to the customer and support teams and contains details relating to supporting services and corresponding SLAs, OLAs, underpinning contracts and suppliers. It also holds details on service costs and, in some cases, charges and revenue.

### Designing technology architectures (SD 3.6.3)  ✔

The result of a good architectural design for Service Management is a simple and clear set of norms and standards which can be used:

- To ensure consistency in the creation of new services

■ To guarantee maximum cohesion with the management systems and tools already in place to support the delivery of services.

For designers, a set of architectures doesn't simply act as a collection of constraints on their design, it describes the expectations of the overall environment in which the design will operate.

An architecture for any system should consider its constituent components; their relationship to each other and how they interact; the relationship between the system and its environment; the design principles that govern its appearance and how it behaves.

*Figure 3.2 Architectural relationships*

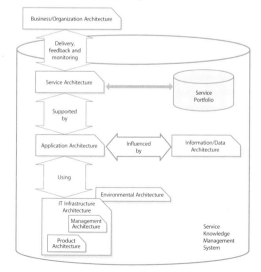

Service Design should consider the technology architecture and its four main components – the data, applications, infrastructure and environment as illustrated in Figure 3.2 – plus the management architecture.

When designing a suitable management architecture consider the following five areas:

- Business requirements
- People, roles and activities
- Processes and procedures
- Management tools
- Technology.

The management architecture needs to be designed top-down to ensure that the overall result is designed with the needs of the business as the key driver for the other areas.

Management architectures need to be business-aligned, not technology-driven.

### Designing processes (SD 3.6.4) ✔

Each organization needs to take a formalized approach to designing processes that are tailored and appropriate to the organization.

A process model enables understanding and helps to articulate the distinctive features of a process.

Each process is owned by a Process Owner, who is responsible for the process, its improvement and for ensuring it meets its objectives.

Process outputs are expected to conform to operational norms, and where this is the case the process can be considered to be effective. If the activities are carried out with a minimum amount of resources the process can be considered efficient.

Process performance and outputs need to be continually reviewed by the Process Owner; emerging requirements and objectives or the availability of new tools need to be taken into account; and actions identified to develop and maintain a process improvement plan.

### Design of measurement systems and metrics (SD 3.6.5) ✔

To effectively manage processes and their outcomes they have to be measured. The measurements and metrics selected need to reflect the goals and objectives of the process being measured.

Process measurements need to be appropriate to the level of capability and maturity of the processes being measured. Immature processes are incapable of supporting sophisticated measurements.

Take care when selecting measurements as they will drive behavioural changes in the organization. Selection of the wrong metric can lead to undesired changes in behaviour, in contradiction to the goals and objectives of the process.

Where possible, metrics need to be driven by organizational goals and developed to operate in a hierarchical way – a metrics tree – so that detailed technical operational and process metrics, at the lowest levels, can be aggregated and reported at a higher level to demonstrate service performance against SLAs. These can then be aggregated to the next level to produce a management dashboard, giving an overall picture of performance. This information can then be used at a higher level again to demonstrate performance against organizational goals and objectives. The Balanced Scorecard is an example of a tool that can be used to develop a set of organizational metrics and measures in this way.

### 3.3.1.5    Design constraints (SD 3.8)

Any design is constrained by a number of external factors; typically these are financial and timescale constraints. Service Design recognizes that all relevant constraints must be understood and considered when determining the optimum design solution. Other examples of constraints may be those imposed as a result of good corporate governance or in adherence to regulatory compliance or external standards, as indicated in Figure 3.3.

*Figure 3.3 Design driven by constraints*

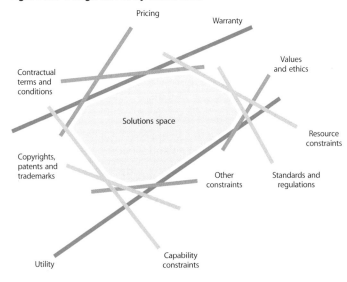

### 3.3.1.6   Roles (SD 6.4)   ✗

Service Design Manager responsibilities include:

- Ensuring service strategies are reflected in the Service Design practice
- Ensuring service designs are produced to meet business requirements
- Producing high-quality, secure and resilient designs for new or changed services
- Producing and maintaining all design documentation, including designs, plans, architectures and policies
- Measuring the effectiveness and efficiency of the Service Design process.

IT Planner responsibilities include:

- Developing IT plans that meet the IT requirements of the business
- Coordinating, measuring and reviewing the implementation progress of all IT strategies and plans
- Producing and maintaining the overall set of IT standards, policies, plans and strategies
- Assuming full responsibility for the management, planning and coordination of IT systems and services.

IT Designer/Architect responsibilities include:

- Producing and reviewing the designs of all new or changed services
- Maintaining a process map of all processes and their high-level interfaces
- Designing secure and resilient technology architectures
- Ensuring that the design of processes, roles and responsibilities is regularly reviewed for effectiveness and efficiency
- Designing the Service Portfolio

■ Designing measurement systems to support continual improvement of service provision.

### 3.3.2  Service Catalogue Management (SD 4.1) ✔

#### Definition: Service Catalogue ✔

A database or structured document with information about all live IT services, including those available for deployment. The Service Catalogue is the only part of the Service Portfolio published to customers, and is used to support the sale and delivery of IT services. The Service Catalogue includes information about deliverables, prices, contact points, ordering and request processes.

### 3.3.2.1   Objectives ✔, scope ✘ and value ✘

The Service Catalogue is a single source of consistent information on all of the agreed services. The objective of Service Catalogue Management is to manage the information contained within the Service Catalogue and to ensure that it is accurate and current.

The scope is to provide and maintain accurate information on all services that are being transitioned, or have been transitioned, to the live environment.

The Service Catalogue provides the business with an accurate, consistent picture of the IT services in use, how they are intended to be used, the business processes they enable and the associated service levels.

### 3.3.2.2   Basic concepts ✔

The Service Catalogue is part of the Service Portfolio. The Service Catalogue contains details of all services from the point they are 'chartered' as part of the Service Strategy stage. It contains details of services as they progress through the design, transition and operation stages of the Service Lifecycle.

The Service Catalogue is also used by many other Service Management processes to support their activities and to provide the basis for analysis across the full scope of delivered services.

The Service Catalogue has two aspects:

- **Business Service Catalogue** ✔: contains details of the IT services delivered, links to the business processes they support and provides the customer view of the Service Catalogue
- **Technical Service Catalogue** ✔: contains details of the IT services delivered, links to the supporting services and Configuration Items (CIs) necessary to deliver the service, underpins the Business Service Catalogue and is not part of the customer view.

### 3.3.2.3   Activities ✘

Key activities for Service Catalogue Management are:

- Agree and document service definitions
- Interface with Service Portfolio Management to agree the contents of the Service Portfolio and the Service Catalogue
- Produce and maintain the Service Catalogue
- Interface with the business to understand the links between business processes and the IT services
- Interface with support teams to understand the relationships with supporting services and CIs.

### 3.3.2.4   Challenges  ✗

The main challenge is in maintaining the Service Catalogue, at the business and technical levels, to ensure that it is current and consistent.

Key to overcoming that challenge are:

■ Education about the benefits to be gained from an accurate and up-to-date Service Catalogue
■ Buy-in at the senior management level.

### 3.3.2.5   Key metrics  ✗

■ Number of IT services recorded and managed within the Service Catalogue as a percentage of those being delivered and transitioned in the live environment
■ Number of variances detected between the information contained within the Service Catalogue and the 'real-world' situation.

### 3.3.2.6   Roles (SD 6.4.5)  ✗

Service Catalogue Manager responsibilities include:

■ Ensuring that all operational services and all services being prepared are recorded in the Service Catalogue
■ Ensuring that all information in the Service Catalogue is accurate and up to date
■ Ensuring that all information in the Service Catalogue is consistent with that in the Service Portfolio
■ Ensuring that the information in the Service Catalogue is adequately protected and backed up.

### 3.3.3  Service Level Management (SD 4.2) ✔

### 3.3.3.1   Objectives ✔, scope ✘ and value ✘

The objectives of Service Level Management (SLM) are to:

- Define, document, agree, monitor, measure, report and review the level of IT services provided
- Ensure that an agreed level of service is provided for all IT services and that the services and their performance are measured in a consistent way.

Service Level Management acts to represent the service provider to the business and the business to the service provider.

It manages the expectations and perceptions of the business, customers and users, and ensures that the service provided is in line with those expectations. Its focus extends beyond currently delivered services to involvement in the design of new or changed services, producing and agreeing the Service Level Requirements for these services.

Service Level Management provides a reliable communication channel and a trusted relationship between the customers and business representatives. It supplies the business with agreed service targets and the required management information to ensure those targets have been met.

### 3.3.3.2   Basic concepts ✔

Service Level Requirements

Service Level Requirements (SLRs) define the customer requirements for an IT service based on business objectives, and are used to negotiate Service Level Agreements.

### Definition: Service Level Agreement ✔

A Service Level Agreement (SLA) is an agreement between an IT service provider and a customer. The SLA describes the IT service, records service level targets, and specifies the responsibilities of the IT service provider and the customer. A single SLA may cover multiple IT services or multiple customers.

Service Level Agreements provide the basis for managing the relationship between the service provider and the customer.

Service Level Management develops SLAs for all services and ensures the service continues to be delivered in line with the agreements made in the SLA.

### Service Level Agreement Monitoring chart

A Service Level Agreement Monitoring (SLAM) chart monitors and reports achievements against service level targets. Such a chart is typically colour-coded to show whether each agreed service level target has been met, missed or nearly missed during each of the previous 12 months.

### Service Level Agreement frameworks

When designing SLA frameworks, options available include:

- **Service-based SLAs**: the SLA describes a specific IT service to be delivered
- **Customer-based SLAs**: all IT services delivered to a specific customer are described
- **Multi-level SLAs**: for example, from corporate down through customer to service, where the agreements at each level are inherited by those at the next. This helps with ongoing

maintenance, making the SLAs easier to work with. The information at the higher levels is subject to less frequent change and is not repeated in every lower-level SLA.

Where service delivery relies on supporting services provided either by other departments or by external suppliers, Service Level Management ensures that OLAs and contracts are in place to underpin the service delivery targets in the Service Level Agreement.

## Definition: Operational Level Agreement ✔

An Operational Level Agreement (OLA) is an agreement between an IT service provider and another part of the same organization. An OLA supports the IT service provider's delivery of IT services to customers. The OLA defines the goods or services to be provided and the responsibilities of both parties.

### Service review

This constitutes meetings held on a regular basis with customers (or their representatives) to review the service achievement in the last period and to preview any issues for the coming period. The customer and provider should be actioned as appropriate to improve weak areas where targets are not being met. Analysis of the cost and impact of service breaches provides valuable input and justification of Service Improvement Plan (SIP) activities and actions.

### Service Improvement Plan

A Service Improvement Plan is a formal plan to implement improvements to a process or service.

### 3.3.3.3   Activities ✔

The key activities for Service Level Management are:

- Design SLA frameworks
- Determine, document and agree requirements for new or changed services and manage them through the Service Lifecycle into SLAs for operational services
- Monitor service performance against SLA
- Collate, measure and improve customer satisfaction
- Produce service reports
- Conduct service reviews and instigate improvements within an overall Service Improvement Plan
- Review and revise SLAs, service scope and underpinning agreements
- Develop underpinning contracts (UC) and relationships
- Manage complaints and compliments.

### 3.3.3.4   Relationships ✔

Interfaces with Service Level Management include:

- Availability Management
  - Provides availability requirements as input to the SLA
  - Reduces SLA breaches due to unavailability

- Capacity Management
  - Provides performance requirements as input to the SLA
  - Reduces SLA breaches due to poor performance

- Change Management
  - Manages changes to SLAs
  - Identifies Projected Service Outages detailing planned variations from SLAs

- Supplier Management
  - Ensures supplier and contractual targets align with SLAs

- Information Security Management
  - Ensures SLAs are developed to align with security policy
- Service Validation and Testing
  - Ensures a new or changed service supports the SLA
- Incident Management
  - Ensures incidents are resolved in line with SLA targets.

### 3.3.3.5    Challenges ✘

- Take care to identify and involve the right people within the customer base when drafting and agreeing the SLA. The manager paying for the service may have very different targets and requirements from the staff who use the service on a day-to-day basis. It is important that all relevant views are gathered and incorporated in the SLA
- If the organization is new to SLM, carefully select an appropriate service to start with. Avoid selecting one that is too complex or 'emotional'
- Remember, this needs to be an agreement on both sides. Ensure appropriate involvement from service delivery staff, especially the key functions within Service Operation.

### 3.3.3.6    Key metrics ✘

- Percentage reduction in SLA targets missed
- Percentage increase in customer satisfaction
- Percentage increase in SLAs agreed against operational services being run
- Percentage increase of SLA reviews completed on time.

### 3.3.3.7    Roles (SD 6.4.6) ✘

Service Level Manager responsibilities include:

- Staying aware of business needs

- Negotiating and agreeing levels of service to be delivered, and formally documenting these agreements in SLAs
- Ensuring that service reports are produced
- Ensuring that service performance reviews are carried out regularly and that agreed actions are progressed
- Definition, recording and communication of all complaints
- Measuring, recording, analysing and improving customer satisfaction.

### 3.3.4   Capacity Management (SD 4.3) ✔

#### 3.3.4.1   Objectives ✔, scope ✗ and value ✗

The objectives of Capacity Management are to:

- Produce and maintain an accurate Capacity Plan, and provide advice and guidance on all capacity- and performance-related issues
- Ensure performance achievements meet or exceed performance targets, and assist with diagnosis and resolution of incidents and problems
- Assess the impact of all changes on the Capacity Plan and proactively improve performance, where cost-effective.

A Capacity Plan is used to manage the resources required to deliver IT services. The plan contains scenarios for different predictions of business demand, and costed options to deliver agreed service level targets.

Capacity Management is a process which extends across the whole Service Lifecycle. A key factor in managing capacity is ensuring it is considered in Service Design. The Capacity Management process provides a focal point for the management of all IT performance and capacity issues.

Capacity Management seeks to understand current and future business and IT needs relating to capacity and performance, and also to understand and take account of current capability and future opportunities presented by advances in technology.

Capacity Management ensures that IT resources are planned and scheduled to deliver a consistent level of service, matched to the agreed current and future needs of the business.

### 3.3.4.2    Basic concepts ✔

Capacity Management is essentially a balancing act:

- Balancing costs against resources needed
- Balancing supply against demand.

Capacity Management is a complex and demanding process. To deliver results it relies on three sub-processes:

- **Business Capacity Management:** translating business needs and plans into requirements for IT services and infrastructure
- **Service Capacity Management:** predicting, managing and controlling the end-to-end performance of the operational IT services and their workloads
- **Component Capacity Management:** predicting, managing and controlling the performance, utilization and capacity of individual IT components.

### 3.3.4.3    Activities ✘

The main activities involved in the Capacity Management process will be carried out in both a reactive and a proactive way. Generally, the more emphasis that is placed on proactive Capacity Management, the less effort that will be required in reacting to incidents and problems due to capacity or performance-related issues.

The main activities of Capacity Management are to:

- **Tune and optimize services, workloads and resources:** including monitoring utilization and response times and analysing the data to identify and implement opportunities to tune the configuration, enabling better use of the available capacity. This also includes opportunities presented through improving resilience or the exploitation of new technology
- **Manage and control thresholds:** including setting and monitoring thresholds at service and component levels. Understanding the workload patterns and their impact on services and components is important when determining appropriate thresholds. Events can be triggered when thresholds are broken and also as a warning when they are at risk of being broken. Controls can be implemented that monitor absolute utilization levels and also significant changes in the rates of utilization
- **Manage demand:** influencing user and customer demand for IT services and so managing the impact on IT resources
- **Model and trend utilization:** including baselining, trend analysis, analytical modelling and simulation modelling, among other techniques
- **Application sizing:** estimating the resource requirements to support a proposed change to an existing service, or the implementation of a new service, to ensure that it meets its required service levels.

### 3.3.4.4   Challenges

- Ensuring the provision of accurate business plans on which to base the Capacity Plan
- Gathering and combining the huge amount of data available in a way that supports the Capacity Management process.

### 3.3.4.5   Key metrics   ✘

■ Percentage accuracy of forecasts of business trends
■ Timely justification and implementation of new technology in line with business requirements
■ Reduction in the business disruption caused by a lack of adequate IT capacity
■ Percentage reduction in the number of SLA breaches due to poor service or component performance.

### 3.3.4.6   Roles (SD 6.4.9)   ✘

Capacity Manager responsibilities include:

■ Ensuring adequate IT capacity to meet current and future levels of service
■ Identifying capacity requirements through discussions with the business
■ Understanding current usage and maximum capacity of IT services and components
■ Production, regular review and revision of the Capacity Plan, identifying current usage and forecast requirements
■ Ensuring appropriate levels of monitoring and thresholds
■ Assessing new technology and its relevance to the organization
■ Ensuring all changes are assessed for their impact on capacity and performance.

### 3.3.5   Availability Management (SD 4.4) ✔

#### Definition: Availability ✔

Availability is the ability of a Configuration Item or IT service to perform its agreed function when required. It is determined by reliability, maintainability, serviceability, performance and security. Availability is usually calculated as a percentage. This calculation is often based on agreed service time and downtime. It is best practice to calculate availability using measurements of the business output of the IT service.

#### 3.3.5.1   Objectives ✔, scope ✗ and value ✗

Service availability is at the core of customer satisfaction and business success. Customer dissatisfaction with the availability of services can be a key factor in losing business to a competitor.

The objectives of Availability Management are to:

- Produce and maintain the Availability Plan, reflecting the current and future needs of the business, and to provide guidance to the business and IT on availability-related issues
- Ensure that availability achievements meet or exceed targets and, where they do not, assist with the diagnosis and resolution of related incidents and problems
- Assess all changes for their impact on the Availability Plan and proactively improve availability, where cost-effective.

Availability Management is key across the whole of the Service Lifecycle. It requires a good understanding of the business needs and how they are translated into service requirements. It has a special focus on the business impact of component or service failure and, as such, is important in the creation and maintenance of the Service Catalogue.

The principles and activities of Availability Management must be applied to the design of all new or significantly changed services as well as being utilized on an ongoing basis to manage the delivery of operational services.

Availability Management ensures that the availability of services matches current and future business needs, and that the business impact of any unavailability is minimized.

### 3.3.5.2    Basic concepts ✔

Availability Management is completed at two interconnected levels:

- **Component availability:** involves all aspects of component availability
- **Service availability:** involves all aspects of service availability and the actual, or potential, service impact of component availability.

Availability Management focuses on the following key aspects which influence the overall availability and the business perception of unavailability:

- **Availability:** the ability to perform an agreed function when required
- **Reliability:** how long an agreed function can be performed without interruption
- **Maintainability:** how quickly and effectively agreed functionality can be returned following an interruption
- **Serviceability:** the ability of a third-party supplier to meet the terms of their contract. This contract will include agreed levels of reliability, maintainability or availability for a Configuration Item.

Availability Management identifies Vital Business Functions (VBFs) and takes these into account when making design recommendations. These recommendations can include designing for:

- **High availability:** to minimize or mask the effect of IT component failure
- **Fault tolerance:** to continue to operate correctly after failure of a component part
- **Continuous operation:** to eliminate planned downtime of an IT service
- **Continuous availability:** to achieve 100% availability – no planned or unplanned downtime.

### 3.3.5.3  Activities ✗

The key activities for Availability Management are:

- Monitor, measure, analyse and report service and component failure
- Unavailability analysis: investigating all events and incidents causing unavailability of services, taking into account time to detect, diagnose, repair, recover and restore service
- Service Failure Analysis: identifying the underlying causes of service interruptions
- Identifying VBFs and designing for availability and recovery
- Component Failure Impact Analysis (CFIA): predicting and evaluating the impact of component failures on service availability
- Single Point of Failure (SPOF): analysing, identifying SPOFs and implementing cost-justifiable countermeasures
- Fault Tree Analysis (FTA): determining the chain of events that can lead to service disruption
- Modelling to determine if new components will meet stated requirements

■ In conjunction with the Change Management process, producing the Projected Service Outage (PSO) document, to detail any planned variations from the service availability agreed in SLAs and to ensure it is communicated to all stakeholders.

### 3.3.5.4   Challenges ✗
■ Meeting the high expectations of the business relating to the availability of services, including any assumptions based on 100% availability as an entry point and also on rapid recovery following a failure
■ The ability to successfully gather and combine the huge amount of data available into a useful Availability Management Information System (AMIS).

### 3.3.5.5   Key metrics ✗
■ Percentage reduction in the unavailability of services and components
■ Percentage reduction in critical time failures, e.g. during peak business usage hours
■ Percentage reduction in cost of unavailability.

### 3.3.5.6   Roles (SD 6.4.7) ✗
Availability Manager responsibilities include:

■ Ensuring that all new and existing services deliver the levels of availability required by the business
■ Assisting with the investigation and diagnosis of incidents and problems that cause unavailability
■ Participating in infrastructure design to specify availability requirements
■ Taking responsibility for monitoring actual availability against agreed targets

- Creating and maintaining the Availability Management Information System (AMIS) and the Availability Plan aiming to deliver required availability and improving overall availability, in a cost justified way, to ensure evolving business requirements can continue to be met
- Managing and maintaining an availability testing schedule for all availability mechanisms
- Assessing all changes for their impact on service availability and the Availability Plan.

### 3.3.6   IT Service Continuity Management (SD 4.5) ✔

### 3.3.6.1   Objectives ✔, scope ✗ and value ✗

The objectives of IT Service Continuity Management (ITSCM) are to:

- Maintain a set of IT Service Continuity Plans and IT recovery plans that support the overall Business Continuity Plans and, in support of this, to carry out regular Business Impact Analysis (BIA), risk analysis and management activities
- Provide advice and guidance on continuity and recovery-related issues
- Assess the impact of all changes on the IT Service Continuity Plans.

ITSCM serves to underpin the activities of the Business Continuity Management (BCM) process and focuses on those events that the business considers to be a 'disaster'. It does not cover minor technical faults which are addressed through the Service Desk and Incident Management processes. These 'minor' issues are also covered by the Availability Management process in the design of services for availability and recovery.

Additionally, ITSCM does not usually directly address longer-term risks such as those from changes in business direction, diversification and restructuring, when there is generally time to evaluate the risks and address them through an IT Change Management programme.

ITSCM is invaluable in supporting the business strategy, as it is driven by business risk as identified by Business Continuity Planning and ensures that recovery arrangements for IT services are aligned to business needs.

### 3.3.6.2    Basic concepts ✔

A lifecycle approach should be adopted in setting up and operating ITSCM. These stages form the foundation for the ITSCM activities, and they are:

- Initiation
- Requirements and strategy
- Implementation
- Ongoing operation.

ITSCM is a cyclical process which ensures continuity and recovery plans exist and that they are continually aligned with the Business Continuity Plans (BCPs) and business priorities. ITSCM should support the strategy and plans produced as a result of a Business Continuity Management (BCM) process.

Business Continuity Plan

A Business Continuity Plan defines the steps required to restore business processes following a disruption. It also identifies triggers for invocation, people to be involved, communications etc. IT Service Continuity Plans form a significant part of Business Continuity Plans.

## Business Continuity Management

This is responsible for managing risks that may seriously impact the business by reducing them to an acceptable level and then planning for the recovery of business processes should a business disruption occur. Business Continuity Management sets the objectives, scope and requirements for ITSCM.

## Business Impact Analysis

This is the activity within Business Continuity Management that identifies Vital Business Functions (VBFs) and their dependencies, which may include suppliers, people, other business processes, IT services etc. Business Impact Analysis defines the recovery requirements for IT services, including recovery time objectives, recovery point objectives and minimum service level targets for each IT service.

## Risk assessment

Assessment is the initial step of risk management, analysing the value of business assets, identifying threats to those assets and evaluating the vulnerability of each asset to the threats. Risk assessments can be quantitative or qualitative.

### 3.3.6.3    Activities

The key activities for ITSCM are illustrated in Figure 3.4.

*Figure 3.4 Lifecycle of Service Continuity Management*

**Lifecycle**

Business Continuity Management (BCM)

Initiation

Requirements and strategy

Business Continuity Strategy

Business Continuity Plans

Implementation

Invocation

Ongoing Operation

**Key activities**
- Policy setting
- Scope
- Initiate a project

- Business Impact Analysis
- Risk Assessment
- IT Service Continuity Strategy

- Develop IT Service Continuity Plans
- Develop IT plans, recovery plans and procedures
- Organization Planning
- Testing strategy

- Education, awareness and training
- Review and audit
- Testing
- Change Management

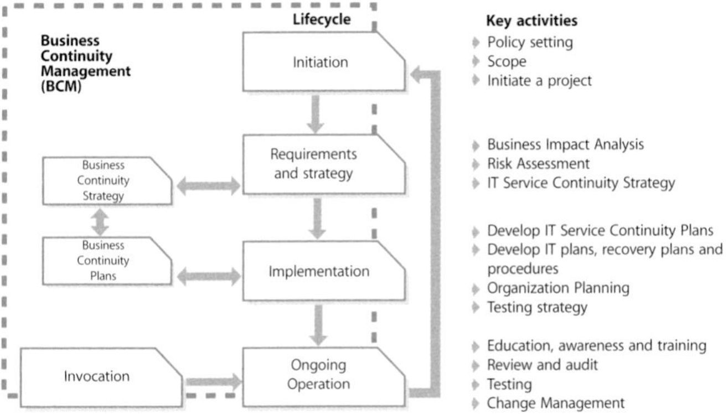

### 3.3.6.4  Challenges ✗
- ■ Developing appropriate ITSCM plans where there is no overall BCM process or plan. In such cases it is usually necessary for IT to educate the business to adopt good practice in this area
- ■ Where IT plans are developed in the absence of business plans they may be inappropriate, and the blame for failure, in the event of a disaster, will be placed on IT.

### 3.3.6.5  Key metrics ✗
- ■ All service recovery targets are agreed and documented and are achievable within the ITSCM plans
- ■ Overall reduction in the assessed risk and impact of possible disasters.

### 3.3.6.6  Roles (SD 6.4.8) ✗
IT Service Continuity Manager responsibilities include:

- Implementing and maintaining the ITSCM process
- Ensuring that ITSCM plans underpin and align with BCM plans
- Developing and maintaining the organization's continuity strategy
- Managing the IT Service Continuity Plan whilst in operation
- Ensuring that all IT service areas are prepared and able to respond to an invocation of the continuity plans
- Assessing all changes for their impact on IT service continuity.

### 3.3.7   Information Security Management (SD 4.6)  ✔

#### 3.3.7.1   Objectives ✔, scope ✘ and value ✘

The objectives for Information Security Management are:

- **Availability:** information is available and usable when required
- **Confidentiality:** information is observed by, or disclosed to, only those who have the right to know
- **Integrity:** information is complete, accurate and protected against unauthorized modification
- **Authenticity and non-repudiation:** business transactions and information exchanges between enterprises, or with partners, can be trusted.

Information Security Management (ISM) is a governance activity within the corporate governance framework. It provides the strategic direction and is the focal point for all security activities. It ensures the objectives are achieved, that information security risks are managed and that enterprise information resources are used responsibly.

The term 'information' includes data stores, databases, metadata and takes into account all channels used to exchange or disclose that information.

ISM needs to understand:

- Business Security Policy and plans
- Current business operation and its security requirements
- Legislative requirements
- Obligations and responsibilities with regard to security contained within SLAs
- Business and IT risks and their management.

ISM ensures an Information Security Policy is maintained and enforced that fulfils the needs of the Business Security Policy and the requirements of corporate governance.

ISM raises awareness across the organization of the need to secure all information assets.

### 3.3.7.2    Basic concepts ✔

The Information Security Framework consists of:

- **Information Security Policy:** authorized by top management in the business and IT, covering all areas of information security and appropriate to meet the Information Security Management objectives
- **Information Security Management System (ISMS):** the basis for the development of a cost-effective information security programme that supports the business objectives. It is focused around five key elements as indicated in Figure 3.5
- **Security strategy**
- **Security organizational structure**
- **Security communications and training strategies and plans**
- **Information Security Management process**, as indicated in section 3.3.7.3.

*Figure 3.5  Framework for managing IT security*

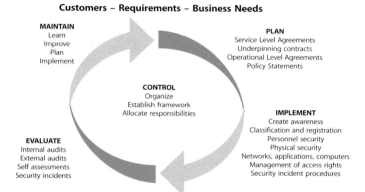

ISO/IEC 27001 is the formal standard against which organizations may seek independent certification of their ISMS.

### 3.3.7.3    Activities ✗

The key activities of Information Security Management are:

■ Produce, review and revise the Information Security Policy
■ Communicate, implement and enforce the security policies
■ Assess and classify all information assets and documentation
■ Implement and improve a set of security controls and risk responses
■ Monitor and manage all security breaches and major security incidents
■ Analyse, report on and take actions to reduce the volumes and impact of security incidents

■ Schedule and undertake security reviews, audits and penetration tests.

### 3.3.7.4    Challenges  ✗

■ Ensuring adequate support for the Information Security Policy from the business – Information Security objectives cannot be met without visible support and endorsement from business top management.

### 3.3.7.5    Key metrics  ✗

■ Percentage decrease in security breaches
■ Increase in the acceptance of, and conformance to, security procedures
■ Increased awareness of the Information Security Policy throughout the organization.

### 3.3.7.6    Roles (SD 6.4.10)  ✗

Security Manager responsibilities include:

■ Developing and maintaining the Information Security Policy
■ Communicating and enforcing the policy
■ Classifying all information assets and appropriate levels of control
■ Monitoring and managing all security breaches and major security incidents
■ Ensuring all changes are assessed for their impact on the Information Security Policy and controls
■ Performing security reviews and tests.

### 3.3.8    Supplier Management (SD 4.7) ✔

#### Definition: Supplier ✔

A third party responsible for supplying goods or services that are required to deliver IT services. Examples of suppliers include commodity hardware and software vendors, network and telecom providers, and outsourcing organizations.

#### 3.3.8.1    Objectives ✔, scope ✘ and value ✘

The objectives of Supplier Management are to:

- Ensure that underpinning contracts and agreements with suppliers are aligned with business needs, and support and align with agreed targets
- Obtain value for money from all suppliers and contracts by:
    - Negotiating and agreeing contracts with suppliers and managing throughout their lifecycle
    - Managing supplier performance and the relationships with the suppliers
- Maintain a supplier policy and a supporting Supplier and Contract Database (SCD).

#### Definition: Contract ✔

A contract is a legally binding agreement between two or more parties.

The Supplier Management process includes all suppliers and contracts needed to support the IT services. The process recognizes the supplier's value contribution and builds and manages a relationship that sustains that contribution. The relationship with each supplier is owned by an individual and is reviewed and managed centrally via the Supplier Management process.

Typically, suppliers are involved in some stage of the delivery of an end-to-end service. Where an external business partner or supplier is used, the SLA is supported by an underpinning contract.

The Supplier Management process ensures that all underpinning services supplied externally are appropriate to support the agreed targets and business needs laid out in the SLAs. This ensures delivery of a seamless, end-to-end service to the business.

### 3.3.8.2  Basic concepts ✔

Supplier and Contracts Database

All Supplier Management activities should be guided by supplier strategy and policy from Service Strategy. To achieve consistency and effectiveness in the implementation of the policy, a Supplier and Contracts Database (SCD) needs to be established and maintained. This is used to manage supplier contracts throughout their lifecycle, and contains key details of all contracts with suppliers. Ideally the SCD should form an integrated part of the Service Knowledge Management System (SKMS).

### 3.3.8.3  Activities ✗

Supplier Management activities, including where they are carried out in the Service Lifecycle, are:

- ■ **Service Design:**
    - – Identify business needs and prepare the Business Case
    - – Evaluate and procure new contracts and suppliers
    - – Supplier categorization and maintenance of the SCD

- **Service Transition:**
  - Establish new suppliers and contracts
- **Service Operation:**
  - Supplier contract management and performance
  - Contract renewal or termination.

### 3.3.8.4   Challenges ✗

- Working within an imposed, non-ideal, contract that has poorly defined terms and conditions
- Insufficient expertise retained in the organization
- Losing the strategic perspective, focusing on operational issues, causing a lack of focus on strategic relationship objectives.

### 3.3.8.5   Key metrics ✗

- Increase in the number of suppliers meeting the targets within the contract
- Increase in the number of supplier and contractual targets aligned with the SLA and SLR targets
- Reduction in the number of service breaches caused by suppliers
- Increase in the number of suppliers with nominated supplier managers.

### 3.3.8.6   Roles (SD 6.4.11) ✗

Supplier manager responsibilities include:

- Providing assistance in the development and review of SLAs, contracts and agreements
- Ensuring that value for money is obtained from all IT suppliers and contracts
- Ensuring that all IT supplier processes are consistent with corporate strategy and processes

- Maintaining and reviewing the SCD
- Ensuring that underpinning contracts are aligned with SLAs and the needs of the business
- Ensuring that roles and relationships between lead and sub-contracted suppliers are documented, maintained and subject to contractual agreement
- Ensuring that effective Supplier Management processes are maintained.

## 3.4 TECHNOLOGY CONSIDERATIONS (SD 7) ✓

The use of Service Management tools is essential to the success of most process implementations. Tools requirements for processes across the lifecycle stages can be found in each of the core publications.

- **Do** use tools to support and enhance (not replace) your assets, i.e. resources and capabilities
- **Do** implement tools to support processes, not the other way around
- **Do not** limit tools requirements to functionality
- **Do not** assume purchasing a tool will solve all of your problems.

### 3.4.1 Integrated Service Management technology requirements (SO 7.1) ✗

To be fully effective, the technology supporting any process implementation needs to be integrated. The following core functionality underpins integrated Service Management technology:

- Self-help
- Workflow or process engine

- Integrated Configuration Management System
- Discovery/deployment/licensing technology
- Remote control
- Diagnostic utilities
- Reporting
- Dashboards
- Integration with Business Service Management.

### 3.4.2  Service automation (SS 8.1)  ✔

The automation of service processes can improve the utility and warranty of the service by:

- Improving service quality
- Reducing costs
- Reducing complexity and uncertainty
- Efficiently resolving trade-offs.

In reducing complexity and uncertainty, automation improves the warranty of services and the supporting processes by responding in a timely and consistent way to specific triggers, and reducing the variability of output of the process or activity. As a result, an automated process can offer simple and predictable input to other dependent processes.

In this way service automation can assist with integrating Service Management processes.

### 3.4.3  Challenges  ✘

Care should be taken when planning to apply automation:

- Simplify the service processes
- Clarify activity flows, task allocations, information needs and interactions

- Protect users from the complexities of the underlying system and technology
- Avoid automating complex, non-standard or unusual tasks.

# 4    Service Transition

Service Transition moves services and service changes into operational use. Service Transition achieves this by receiving a new or changed Service Design Package (SDP) from the Service Design stage, testing it to ensure it meets the needs of the business, and deploying it within the production environment.

## 4.1    GOALS, OBJECTIVES, SCOPE AND VALUE (ST 1.3, 2.4)

### 4.1.1    Goals  ✔

The goals for Service Transition are to:

- ■ Transition services to and from the live environment, managing required resources and risks and ensuring that agreed warranty and utility are delivered
- ■ Set customer expectations of how the performance and use of a new or changed service can be used to enable business change
- ■ Ensure that the service can be used in accordance with the requirements and constraints specified within the service requirements, reducing variations in the predicted and actual performance of the transitioned services, reducing known errors, and minimizing risks
- ■ Enable the business change project or customer to integrate a release into their business processes and services.

### 4.1.2    Objectives  ✔

The main objectives for Service Transition are to:

■ Plan and manage the resources to successfully establish a new or changed service into production within the predicted cost, quality and time estimates
■ Ensure there is minimal unpredicted impact on the production services, operations and support organization
■ Increase proper use of the services and underlying applications and technology solutions.

### 4.1.3  Scope ✗

The scope of Service Transition includes the management and coordination of the resources to package, build, test and deploy a release into production and to establish the new or changed service as specified by the customer and stakeholder requirements. Service Transition also manages the transfer of services to or from external service providers.

### 4.1.4  Value to business ✔

Effective Service Transition provides the following benefits:

■ Enables high volumes of change and release for the business
■ An understanding of the level of risk during and after change, e.g. service outage, disruption
■ Aligns new or changed services with the customer's business requirements
■ Ensures that customers and users can use the new or changed service effectively.

## 4.2    KEY PRINCIPLES (ST 3.1) ✗

■ The nature of the services needs to be clearly understood: the utility and warranty (see section 2.2.3) that have been defined, and the assets that are required to deliver them

- Although service levels may be degraded, the utility of a service can continue to be delivered during major disruptions or disasters.

## 4.3    PROCESSES AND ACTIVITIES

### 4.3.1    Transition Planning and Support (ST 4.1)  ✗

#### 4.3.1.1    Objectives ✗, scope ✗ and value ✗

The objectives of Transition Planning and Support are to:

- Plan and coordinate the resources to successfully deploy a new or changed service into production within the predicted cost, quality and time estimates
- Ensure that all parties adopt standard and re-usable processes and supporting systems
- Provide clear and comprehensive plans that enable customer and business alignment.

Service Transition Planning and Support is also responsible for managing risk and disruptions when transitioning the Service Design Package to Service Operations.

An integrated approach to planning improves the alignment of Service Transition plans with the plans of the customers, suppliers and the business, and can significantly improve a service provider's ability to handle high volumes of change and releases.

#### 4.3.1.2    Basic concepts  ✗

Service Design develops a new or changed service and documents it within a Service Design Package (SDP). The SDP includes key information required by the Service Transition team, including:

- Service Utility and Service Warranty requirements

- Service specifications
- Service models and architectural design
- Definition and design of each release package
- Release and deployment plans
- Service Acceptance Criteria.

### 4.3.1.3   Activities

Key activities for Transition Planning and Support are:

- Define the overall transition strategy, including policy, roles and responsibilities, standards and frameworks, success criteria
- Prepare for Service Transition, including the review, and check inputs (e.g. Service Design Package, evaluation of acceptance criteria), raising Requests for Change, checking transition readiness and baselining the configuration
- Plan and coordinate Service Transition, including production of Service Transition plans, reviewing and coordinating with release and deployment plans
- Provide transition process support, including advice, administration, progress monitoring and reporting.

### 4.3.1.4   Challenges

- Ensuring all change activity is driven through Service Transition
- Balancing the needs of the business against the needs of protecting live service
- Integrating with development and project lifecycles
- Having the appropriate authority and empowerment to execute the processes
- Can be seen as a barrier or over-bureaucratic.

### 4.3.1.5    Key metrics ✘

- Number of releases implemented that meet the customer's agreed requirements in terms of cost, quality, scope and release schedule (expressed as a percentage of all releases)
- Reduced number of issues, risks and delays caused by inadequate planning
- Reduced number of incidents caused by change.

### 4.3.1.6    Roles ✘

The Service Transition Manager is responsible for planning and coordinating the resources to deploy a major release within the predicted cost, time and quality estimates.

## 4.3.2    Change Management (ST 4.2) ✔

### 4.3.2.1    Objectives ✔, scope ✘ and value ✘

The objective of Change Management is to ensure that changes are recorded, evaluated, authorized, prioritized, planned, tested, implemented, documented and reviewed in a controlled manner.

The scope of Change Management covers changes to service assets and Configuration Items across the whole Service Lifecycle – the process addresses all service change.

> **Definition: Service change ✔**
>
> Service change is the addition, modification or removal of anything that could have an effect on IT services. The scope should include all IT services, Configuration Items, processes, documentation etc.

The scope of Change Management applies to all levels of Service Management – strategic, tactical and operational, as illustrated in Figure 4.1.

*Figure 4.1  Scope of Change and Release Management*

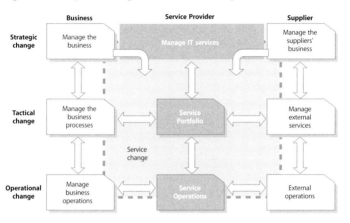

Change Management provides value by promptly evaluating and delivering the changes required by the business, and by minimizing the disruption and re-work caused by failed changes.

### 4.3.2.2   Basic concepts   ✔

Request for Change

A Request for Change (RFC) is a formal request for a change to be made which goes to the Change Advisory Board (CAB) for approval. It includes details of the proposed change and may be recorded on paper or electronically.

Types of change request

A change request is a formal communication requesting change to one or more Configuration Items –for example, an RFC, a Service Desk call or a Project Initiation Document. Different types of change may require different types of change request, each with specific forms and procedures (for example, for impact assessment and change authorization). These procedures need to be appropriate to the scale and profile of the change request type, have defined and unique naming conventions, and be aligned to the stages of the Service Lifecycle impacted, as illustrated in Table 4.1.

Change request types can be categorized as:

- **Normal change** ✔: normal change that goes through the full assessment, authorization and implementation stages
- **Standard change** ✔: pre-approved change that is low risk, relatively common and follows a procedure or work instruction, e.g. a password reset or provision of standard equipment to a new employee. RFCs are not always required to implement a standard change, and they may be logged and tracked using a different mechanism, e.g. a Service Request. Often service operational maintenance changes are standard changes
- **Emergency change** ✔: reserved only for highly critical changes that must be introduced as soon as possible, e.g. changes needed to restore failed high availability or widespread service failure, or changes that will prevent such a failure from imminently occurring. The Change Management process normally has a specific procedure for handling emergency changes.

**Table 4.1 Examples of types of change request by Service Lifecycle stage**

| Type of change | Procedures | Service Strategy | Service Design | Service Transition | Service Operation | Continual Service Improvement |
|---|---|---|---|---|---|---|
| New portfolio item | Service Change Management | ✓ | | | | |
| Service improvement | Service Change Management | ✓ | ✓ | ✓ | ✓ | ✓ |
| Business change project proposal | Project Change Management | | ✓ | ✓ | | ✓ |
| User access request | User access | | | | ✓ | |

## Change Advisory Board

This is a group of people who advise the Change Manager in the assessment, prioritization and scheduling of changes. These boards are usually made up of representatives from all areas within the IT service provider, the business and third parties. CAB members assess both business and technical perspectives.

Change Advisory Boards should:

- Be composed according to the changes being considered
- Vary in make-up even across the range of a single meeting
- Involve suppliers when useful
- Reflect both users' and customers' views
- Include the Problem Manager, Service Level Manager and customer relations staff for at least part of the time.

## Emergency Change Advisory Board

For emergency change there may not be time to convene the full CAB, so it is necessary to identify a smaller board with authority to make emergency decisions, i.e. an Emergency Change Advisory Board (ECAB).

Change procedures should specify how the composition of the CAB and ECAB will be determined in each instance.

## Remediation planning

A change should not be approved without having first identified what to do if it is not successful. Where possible, a back-out plan should be provided to recover the organization to its original or a known state should the change fail, e.g. reloading a baselined set of Configuration Items, re-visiting the change itself or, if severe, invoking the organization's Business Continuity Plan. Only by considering remediation options available prior to instigating a change and establishing that the remediation is viable, can the risk of the proposed change be determined and the appropriate decisions taken.

## Change schedule

This schedule lists all approved changes and planned dates. It becomes an important audit trail to support Incident/Problem Management among other processes.

## Change process models and workflows

A change process model is a repeatable way of dealing with a particular type of change. A change process model sets out specific pre-defined steps that are followed for a specific type of change. Support tools can be used to automate the handling, management, reporting and escalation of the process. The change process model includes:

- Steps to handle the change including handling issues and unexpected events
- The chronological order in which to take the steps, with any dependencies or co-processing defined
- Responsibilities: who should do what
- Timescales and thresholds for completion of the actions
- Escalation procedures: who should be contacted and when.

The seven Rs of Change Management ✔

The following questions must be answered for all changes:

- Who **raised** the change?
- What is the **reason** for the change?
- What is the **return** required from the change?
- What are the **risks** involved in the change?
- What **resources** are required to deliver the change?
- Who is **responsible** for the build, test and implementation of the change?
- What is the **relationship** between this change and other changes?

Without this information, an impact assessment cannot be completed, and the balance of risk and benefit to the live service cannot be understood. This may result in the change failing to deliver all the possible or expected business benefits or even having a detrimental, unexpected effect on the live service.

### 4.3.2.3   Activities ✔

The key activities of Change Management are:

- Planning and controlling change
- Understanding the impact of change
- Change decision making and change authorization
- Change and release scheduling
- Communication with stakeholders

- Ensuring that there are remediation plans
- Measurement and control
- Management reporting
- Continual improvement.

Typical activities in managing individual changes are:

- Create and record the RFC: the change is raised by the individual or organizational group that requires the change
- Assess and evaluate the change:
  - Establish who should be involved in the assessment and authorization
  - Assess and evaluate the business justification, impact, cost, benefits and risk of changes (see seven Rs above)
- Authorize the change if appropriate
- Communicate the decision to all stakeholders, in particular the initiator of the RFC
- Coordinate change implementation
- Review and close the RFC: evaluate the success or otherwise of the change and any lessons learned.

### 4.3.2.4    Relationships ✔

Interfaces with Change Management include:

- Organizational-level processes
  - Integration with business change processes to ensure change issues, aims and impacts are exchanged
  - Programme and project management need to align to service change
  - Sourcing and partnering require effective Change Management to manage relationships
- Asset and Configuration Management
  - Enables change impact assessment and tracking of change workflow

- – CMS may identify related CIs affected by a change but not included in the original request
- Problem Management
  - – Changes are often required to implement workaround and fix known errors
- IT Service Continuity Management
  - – IT Service Continuity Plans need to be updated via Change Management
- Security Management
  - – Changes required by security are under Change Management
- Capacity and Demand Management
  - – Capacity Management needs to assess impact of changes on capacity
  - – Changes required by Capacity Management are under Change Management.

### 4.3.2.5   Challenges  ✗
- Inaccurate configuration details leading to poor evaluation and higher risk of change failure
- An over-bureaucratic process that hinders effective operation of IT and its services
- Bypassing the process (especially if seen to be bureaucratic)
- Too many emergency changes
- Accountability for changes not clearly defined leading to poor quality and compliance
- Balance between stable production and being responsive to business needs.

### 4.3.2.6   Key metrics  ✗
- Number of changes implemented which meet the customer's agreed requirements

- Reduction in the number of disruptions to services, defects and re-work caused by inaccurate specification, poor or incomplete impact assessment
- Reduction in the number of unauthorized changes
- Reduction in the number and percentage of unplanned changes and emergency fixes
- Change success rate (percentage of changes deemed successful at review/number of RFCs approved)
- Percentage of incidents attributable to changes.

### 4.3.2.7  Roles ✘

Change Manager responsibilities include:

- Managing the quality, review, assessment and approval of RFCs
- Chairing the CAB
- Acting as key liaison between initiators and approvers of changes.

### 4.3.3  Service Asset and Configuration Management (ST 4.3) ✔

#### 4.3.3.1  Objectives ✔, scope ✘ and value ✘

The objective of Service Asset and Configuration Management (SACM) is to define and control the components of services and infrastructure, and to maintain accurate configuration information on the historical, planned and current state of these components, services and infrastructure.

**Asset Management** covers service assets across the whole Service Lifecycle. It provides a complete inventory of assets and states who is responsible for their control. It includes full lifecycle management of IT and service assets, from the point of acquisition through to disposal and maintenance of the asset inventory.

**Configuration Management** provides a configuration model of the services, assets and infrastructure by recording the relationships between service assets and Configuration Items. The scope covers interfaces to internal and external service providers where there are assets and Configuration Items that need to be controlled, e.g. shared assets.

Differences between Service Asset Management and Configuration Management:

- Service Asset Management is the tracking and reporting of the value and ownership of service assets
- Configuration Management is the maintaining of information about Configuration Items (CIs) including their relationships in the Configuration Management System (CMS).

SACM optimizes the performance of service assets and configurations and therefore improves the overall performance of the service, and minimizes the costs and risks caused by poorly managed assets, e.g. service outages, fines, incorrect licence fees and failed audits.

### 4.3.3.2   Basic concepts ✔

#### Definition: Configuration Item ✔

A Configuration Item (CI) is any component that needs to be managed in order to deliver an IT service. Information about each CI is recorded in a configuration record within the Configuration Management System and is maintained throughout its lifecycle by Configuration Management. CIs are under the control of Change Management. CIs typically include IT services, hardware, software, buildings, people and formal documentation such as process documentation and SLAs. CIs should be selected using established selection criteria, grouped, classified and identified in such a way that they are manageable and traceable throughout the Service Lifecycle.

#### Definition: Configuration Management System ✔

A Configuration Management System (CMS) is a set of tools and databases used to manage an IT service provider's configuration data. The CMS also includes information about incidents, problems, known errors, changes and releases, and may contain data about employees, suppliers, locations, business units, customers and users. The CMS includes tools for collecting, storing, managing, updating and presenting data about all Configuration Items and their relationships. The CMS is maintained by Configuration Management and is used by all IT Service Management processes.

### Definition: Definitive Media Library ✔

A Definitive Media Library (DML) is one or more locations in which the definitive and approved versions of all software Configuration Items are securely stored. The DML may also contain associated CIs such as licences and documentation. The DML is a single logical storage area even if there are multiple locations. All software in the DML is under the control of Change and Release Management and is recorded in the Configuration Management System. Only software from the DML is acceptable for use in a release.

## Configuration model

A configuration model is a model of the services, assets and infrastructure, including relationships between CIs, that enables other processes to access valuable information (e.g. assessing the impact of incidents, problems and proposed changes; planning and designing new or changed services and their release and deployment; optimizing asset utilization and costs).

## Configuration Management Database

The Configuration Management Database (CMDB) stores configuration records containing attributes of CIs and their relationships. A CMS may include one or more CMDBs.

## Configuration baseline

A configuration baseline is the configuration of a service, product or infrastructure that has been formally reviewed and agreed upon, which thereafter serves as the basis for further activities and can be changed only through formal change procedures. A configuration baseline can be used as a checkpoint, a service development milestone, a basis for future

builds and changes, to assemble components for a change or
release or to provide the basis for a configuration audit or
back-out.

### 4.3.3.3 Activities ✔

The key activities of SACM are:

- **Management and planning:** the level of Configuration
  Management required for a service or a change project
- **Configuration identification:** defining CI types, naming
  conventions etc.
- **Configuration control:** ensuring there are adequate control
  mechanisms over CIs while maintaining a record of changes
  to CIs, versions, location and ownership
- **Status accounting and reporting:** maintaining the status
  of CIs as progress through their discrete states, e.g.
  Development, Approved, Withdrawn
- **Verification and audit:** checking that the physical CIs exist
  and that documentation is accurate
- **Information management:** backup copies of the CMS should
  be taken regularly and securely stored. It is advisable for one
  copy to be stored at a remote location for use in the event of
  a disaster.

### 4.3.3.4 Relationships ✔

Interfaces with Service Asset and Configuration Management
include:

- Change Management
  - Identifies the impact of proposed changes
- Financial Management
  - Captures key financial information
- IT Service Continuity Management
  - Awareness of assets that the business depends on
  - Control of key spare assets and software

■ Incident and Problem Management
  – Provides and maintains key diagnostic information
  – Maintains and provides data to the Service Desk
■ Availability Management
  – Supports detection of points of failure.

### 4.3.3.5  Challenges ✗
■ Persuading technical support staff of the value of SACM as it may be seen as a hindrance
■ Funding of SACM, as it is not visible to the business
■ Over-engineering and collecting too much data
■ CMS can become out of date as CIs are moved or changes are made.

### 4.3.3.6  Key metrics ✗
■ Ratio of used licences against paid for licences (should be close to 100%)
■ Accuracy in budgets and charges for the assets utilized by each customer or business unit
■ Percentage reduction in business impact of outages and incidents caused by poor Asset and Configuration Management
■ Reduction in the use of unauthorized hardware and software, non-standard and variant builds that increase complexity, support costs and risk to the business services.

### 4.3.3.7  Roles ✗
■ Service Asset Manager: manages the lifecycle of assets
■ Configuration Manager: manages the lifecycle and relationships of all CIs
■ Configuration Analyst: analyses/proposes scope of asset and configuration processes, undertakes process activities
■ Configuration Admin/Librarian: controls the receipt, identification, storage and withdrawal of all supported CIs

■ CMS/Tools Administrator: monitors the performance and capacity of Asset and Configuration Management systems and recommends improvement opportunities.

### 4.3.4 Knowledge Management (ST 4.7) ✔

#### 4.3.4.1 Objectives ✔, scope ✘ and value ✘

The ability to deliver a quality service or process is impacted by the ability of those involved to respond to circumstances based on their understanding of the situation, the options, and the consequences and benefits, i.e. their knowledge of the situation they are or may find themselves in.

The quality and relevance of the knowledge depends on the accessibility, quality and continued relevance of the underpinning data and information available to service staff.

The objectives of Knowledge Management are to gather, analyse, store and share knowledge and information within an organization. The primary purpose is to improve efficiency by reducing the need to rediscover knowledge.

Knowledge Management ensures that the right person has the right knowledge, at the right time, to deliver and support the services required by the business. This results in:

■ More efficient services with improved quality
■ Clear and common understanding of the value provided by services
■ Relevant information that is always available.

The scope of Knowledge Management includes oversight of the management of knowledge, the information and data from which that knowledge is derived, across the Service Lifecycle.

Knowledge Management is typically displayed within the Data-to-Information-to-Knowledge-to-Wisdom (DIKW) structure as illustrated in Figure 4.2.

The ability to deliver a quality service or process depends on the ability of those involved to respond to circumstances – and that depends heavily on their understanding of the situation, the options and the consequences and benefits. Effective Knowledge Management is a powerful asset for people in all roles across all stages of the Service Lifecycle.

*Figure 4.2 Flow from data to wisdom*

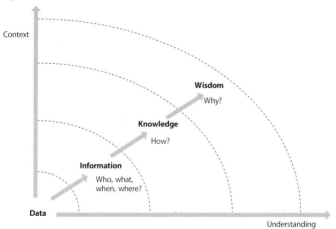

### 4.3.4.2    Basic concepts ✔
Data-to-Information-to-Knowledge-to-Wisdom

■ **Data:** a set of discrete facts about events

- **Information** (who, what, when, where?): processing and adding context to the data
- **Knowledge** (how?): knowledge is created by using the information for action and answers the question 'how'
- **Wisdom** (why?): wisdom is the ability to use knowledge in a way that improves outcomes.

Definition: Service Knowledge Management System ✔

The Service Knowledge Management System (SKMS) is a set of tools and databases used to manage knowledge and information. The SKMS includes the Configuration Management System, as well as other tools and databases. The SKMS stores, manages, updates and presents all information that an IT service provider needs to manage the full lifecycle of IT services.

Service Knowledge Management System

The Service Knowledge Management System is underpinned by the Configuration Management System (CMS) and the Configuration Management Database (CMDB) but in its wider context it also holds knowledge from other sources such as:

- The experience of staff
- Records of peripheral matters (weather, user numbers and behaviours, market conditions)
- Suppliers, and partner requirements, abilities and skills
- User skill levels (e.g. use of PCs or the Internet).

*Figure 4.3  Relationship of the CMDB, CMS and the SKMS*

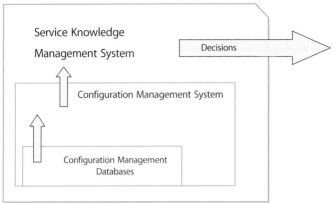

Figure 4.3 is a very simplified illustration of the relationship of the three levels of data and how they support the business in making informed decisions.

### 4.3.4.3  Activities ✗

The key activities of Knowledge Management are:

■ **Define Knowledge Management strategy:** an overall strategy is required including how to identify, capture and maintain knowledge
■ **Knowledge transfer:** retrieving and sharing knowledge in order to solve problems and support dynamic learning, strategic planning and decision making
■ **Evaluation and improvement:** measure the use made of the data, evaluate its usefulness, and identify improvements.

#### 4.3.4.4    Challenges  ✗
- Understanding what knowledge is necessary to support the decisions that must be made
- Understanding which conditions need to be monitored (changing external and internal circumstances, ranging from end-user demand, legal requirements through to weather forecasts)
- The cost of capturing and maintaining data, and the value that data may bring, bearing in mind the negative impact of data overload on effective knowledge transfer
- Intellectual property rights and copyright issues.

#### 4.3.4.5    Key metrics  ✗
- Reduced time and effort required to support and maintain services
- Reduced time to find information for diagnosis and resolving incidents and problems
- Reduced dependency on personnel for knowledge.

#### 4.3.4.6    Roles  ✗
Knowledge Manager responsibilities include:

- Ensuring that the service provider is able to gather, analyse, store and share knowledge and information
- Improving efficiency by reducing the need to rediscover knowledge.

### 4.3.5    Release and Deployment Management (ST 4.4)  ✔

#### 4.3.5.1    Objectives  ✔, scope  ✗ and value  ✗
The objective of Release and Deployment Management is to build, test and deliver new or changed services into the production environment, within required timescales and with minimal disruption to existing services. The new service and

supporting systems should be capable of being operated successfully and should deliver the agreed service requirements (utility and warranty).

The scope of Release and Deployment Management includes the processes, systems and functions required to package, build, test and deploy a release into production in accordance with the Service Design Package (SDP). This includes handover to the Service Operation lifecycle stage.

Effective Release and Deployment Management adds value by ensuring that customers and users can use the new or changed service in a way that supports the business, and by delivering change faster, at optimum cost and with minimal risk. Well-planned and implemented release and deployment can make a significant difference to an organization's service costs by minimizing troubleshooting and re-work.

### 4.3.5.2   Basic concepts ✔

#### Definition: Release Unit ✔

A Release Unit comprises the components of an IT service that are normally released together. It typically includes sufficient components to perform a useful function. For example one Release Unit could be a desktop PC, including hardware, software, licences, documentation etc. A different Release Unit may be the complete Payroll Application, including IT Operations procedures and user training.

## Release policy ✔

A release policy should be defined for services that includes:

- Identification, numbering and naming conventions for each release type and expected frequencies
- Roles and responsibilities within the release and deployment process
- How the configuration baseline for the release is captured and verified against the actual release contents
- Criteria and authority for acceptance of the release at each stage.

### Release identification

All releases must be uniquely identified. The identification scheme needs to be described in the release policy, referencing the affected Configuration Items, and including a version number

### Release package

This describes one or more Release Units required to implement the new or changed service.

### Release Deployment

Deployments can either be Big Bang, i.e. all at once, or phased, i.e. deployed to users in stages and at different times.

A release can be 'pushed' whereby the service component is deployed from the centre and pushed out to the target; or 'pulled' whereby users are free to initiate the deployment when required. Mechanisms to release and deploy can be manual or automated.

## 4.3.5.3 Activities ✗

The key activities of Release and Deployment Management are:

- **Planning**: select the most appropriate release and deployment plans, and agree with customers and stakeholders. Define entry and exit criteria for each step in the process
- **Build**: assemble and integrate the release components
- **Service testing and pilots**: test service requirements and operational requirements
- **Plan and prepare** for deployment
- **Deploy service and supporting processes**: including required user and technical training
- **Retire/decommission any unused assets**: remove unused assets, e.g. hardware and software
- **Verify deployment**: verify that users, Service Operations, other staff and stakeholders are capable of using or operating the service, identify any issues and take corrective action.

Early-life support

Once a new or changed service has been deployed into the production environment, Service Transition may provide early-life support for a limited period of time. During early-life support the service levels and monitoring thresholds will be reviewed and additional resources may be provided for Incident and Problem Management.

The service V-model

An approach to testing used by the Release and Deployment Management process, and the Service Validation and Testing process. The service V-model provides a framework to organize the levels of Configuration Items to be managed through the lifecycle and the associated Validation and Testing activities to be undertaken. As illustrated in Figure 4.4, the left side represents the specifications of the service requirements down to a detailed

Service Design. The right side focuses on the Validation and Testing activities that are performed against each of the specifications defined on the left.

*Figure 4.4 Example service V-model*

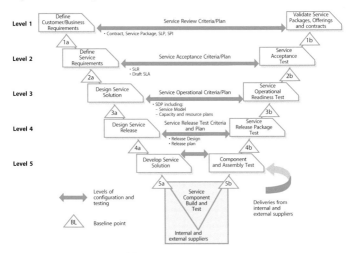

### 4.3.5.4   Challenges

- Ensuring planned project delivery dates are achievable
- Understanding the stakeholder perspectives
- Understanding the risks
- Pragmatic approach to the challenges of delivery
- Establishing standard performance metrics for all transitions.

### 4.3.5.5   Key metrics

- Reduced variance from service performance required by customers

- Reduced number of incidents for the service
- Increased customer and user satisfaction with the services delivered
- Reduced resources and costs to diagnose and fix incidents and problems in deployment and production
- Reduced discrepancies in configuration audits compared with the real world.

### 4.3.5.6 Roles

Release Packaging and Build Manager responsibilities include:

- Establishing the final release configuration and building the final release
- Testing the release and publishing known errors and workarounds.

Deployment Manager responsibilities include:

- Planning, scheduling and controlling the movement of releases to test and live environments
- Ensuring that the integrity of the live environment is protected and that the correct components are released.

### 4.3.6 Service Validation and Testing (ST 4.5)

### 4.3.6.1 Objectives, scope and value

The objective of Service Validation and Testing is to ensure that a new or changed service and its associated release process will meet the needs of the business (utility and warranty) at the agreed cost.

Service Validation and Testing can be applied throughout the Service Lifecycle to quality assure any aspect of a service, and should cover the complete end-to-end service including both internally and externally developed service components.

Service Validation provides value by preventing service failures that can harm the service provider's business and the customer's assets, which can result in outcomes such as loss of reputation, loss of money, loss of time, injury and death.

### 4.3.6.2   Basic concepts ✗

The key purpose of Service Validation and Testing is to provide objective evidence that the new or changed service supports the business requirements, including the agreed SLAs. The service is tested explicitly against the utility and warranty set out in the Service Design Package, including business functionality, availability, continuity, security, usability and regression testing.

- **Test model definition**: specifies, in detail, how the release is to be tested and quality-assured. In particular, this process defines the testing concept and specific test cases to be used during Service Validation
- **Service Design Validation**: ensures that an IT service meets its functionality and quality requirements and that the service provider is ready to operate the new service when it has been deployed
- **Release test**: tests all release components and all tools and mechanisms required for deployment, migration and back-out. This process ensures that only components that meet stringent quality criteria are deployed into the live environment
- **Service acceptance testing**: verifies whether all conditions have been met for the new service to be activated, and obtains a binding consent from the customer that the new service fulfils the agreed Service Level Requirements
- **Service Acceptance Criteria**: set of criteria used to ensure that an IT service meets its functionality and quality requirements and that the IT service provider is ready to operate the new IT service when it has been deployed

■ **The service V-model**: see Release and Deployment Management, section 4.3.5.

### 4.3.6.3   Activities ✗

The testing process is shown schematically in Figure 4.5.

The test activities are not undertaken in a sequence. Several activities may be done in parallel, e.g. test execution begins before all the test design is complete.

*Figure 4.5  Example of a validation and testing process*

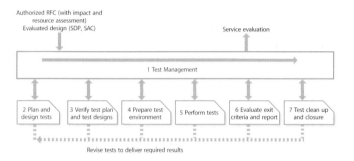

### 4.3.6.4   Challenges ✗
■ Maintaining tests environments and data that match the live environment
■ Insufficient resources to deliver suitable testing
■ Completion of adequate testing as project delivery times come under pressure.

### 4.3.6.5    Key metrics ✗

- Effort required to find defects – i.e. number of defects (by significance, type, category etc.) compared with testing resource applied
- Reduction of repeat errors – feedback from testing ensures that corrective action within design and transition (through CSI) prevents mistakes from being repeated in subsequent releases or services
- Percentage incidents linked to errors detected during testing and released into live environment
- Number and percentage of errors that could have been discovered in testing
- Testing incidents found as percentage of incidents occurring in live operations
- Inspection and testing return on investment (ROI).

### 4.3.6.6    Roles ✗

Test Manager responsibilities include:

- Ensuring that deployed releases and the resulting services meet customer expectations
- Verifying that IT operations are able to support the new service.

### 4.3.7    Evaluation (ST 4.6) ✗

### 4.3.7.1    Objectives ✗, scope ✗ and value ✗

Evaluation is a generic process that considers whether the performance of something is acceptable, value for money, fit for purpose and whether implementation can proceed based on defined and agreed criteria. The objectives of Evaluation are to:

- Evaluate the intended effects of a service change and as much of the unintended effects as reasonably practical given capacity, resource and organizational constraints
- Provide good-quality outputs from evaluation process so that Change Management can expedite an effective decision about whether a service change is to be approved or not.

The scope includes the evaluation of any new or changed service defined by Service Design, during deployment and before final transition to the production environment.

### 4.3.7.2    Basic concepts

- **Risk management:** analyses the threats and weaknesses that have been, or would be, introduced as a result of the service change. Risk = Likelihood x Impact
- **Evaluation plan:** the agreed approach to evaluating the service change against the agreed acceptance criteria
- **Evaluation report:** provides a risk profile, deviation report, qualification/validation statement and recommendation for Change Management to accept or reject the change
- **Evaluation assessments:** assesses the delivery against the evaluation criteria to ensure they have been satisfied
- **Transition evaluation:** risk assessment of the transition plan prior to implementation of the new or changed service to Service Operations.

### 4.3.7.3    Activities

The activities of the Evaluation process are illustrated in Figure 4.6.

*Figure 4.6 Evaluation process*

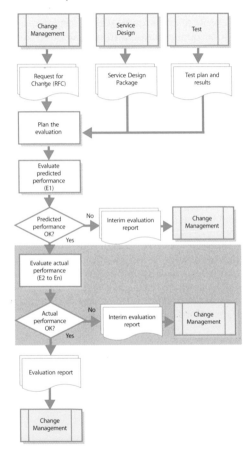

#### 4.3.7.4    Challenges  ✗

- Developing standard performance measures
- Planning subject to estimating by projects
- Understanding stakeholder perspectives
- Balancing the needs of the business and the customer
- Balancing the priorities of the project, service organization and the business.

#### 4.3.7.5    Key metrics  ✗

- Variance from service performance required by customers (minimal and reducing)
- Number of incidents against the service (low and reducing)
- Number of failed designs that have been transitioned
- Cycle time to perform an evaluation (low and reducing).

#### 4.3.7.6    Roles  ✗

Performance and Risk Evaluation Manager responsibilities include:

- Developing the evaluation plan, establishing risk and issues associated with all aspects of the Service Transition
- Providing the evaluation report as input to Change Management.

# 5 Service Operation

Strategic objectives are ultimately realized through Service Operation, requiring effective and efficient delivery and support of IT services to ensure value for the customer and the service provider.

## 5.1 GOALS, OBJECTIVES, SCOPE AND VALUE (SO 2.4)

### 5.1.1 Goals ✔

Service Operation is a critical stage of the Service Lifecycle. All the hard work of Strategy, Design and Transition enables Service Operation to actually deliver the IT services and achieve their agreed Utility and Warranty. Continual improvement is dependent on the monitoring and data gathering carried out during Service Operation.

The main goal of Service Operation is to enable the business to meet its objectives, managing the day-to-day activities whilst maintaining a perspective on the wider context.

### 5.1.2 Objectives ✔

The objectives of Service Operation are to:

- Deliver agreed levels of IT services to the business and customers
- Manage the applications, technology and infrastructure that support delivery of the services
- Support optimization of cost and quality.

### 5.1.3   Scope  ✗

The scope of Service Operation includes operation and management of:

- All aspects of the end-to-end IT services agreed with the business, including aspects done by third parties or the customers and end-users themselves
- Service Management processes that support the IT services
- Technology and infrastructure needed to deliver the IT services
- People who manage the technology, processes and IT services.

### 5.1.4   Value to business  ✔

Service Operation is the stage in the lifecycle where the plans, designs and optimizations are executed and measured. Service Operation is where actual value is seen by the business.

## 5.2   KEY PRINCIPLES

### 5.2.1   Balance in Service Operation (SO 3.2)  ✗

Service Operation has to achieve a balance between many conflicting requirements. Each of these conflicts represents an opportunity for the organization to grow and improve.

- **Internal IT view versus external business view:** the external view is how the IT services are experienced by users and customers. The internal view is how the technology components and systems are managed to deliver the services. An organization that only focuses on business requirements may make promises that cannot be met. An organization that focuses on the internal view only may deliver expensive services with little value

- **Stability versus responsiveness:** an extreme focus on stability may result in business requirements being ignored, an extreme focus on responsiveness may result in unstable and unreliable IT services.
- **Quality of service versus cost of service:** Service Operation must deliver agreed levels of service whilst keeping costs low. Too much focus on cost may result in missing agreed service levels. Too much focus on quality may lead to overspending
- **Reactive versus proactive:** a reactive organization waits for events before it does anything. A proactive organization is always looking for ways to improve. An organization that is too reactive may suffer unplanned service interruptions and poor service quality. An organization that is too proactive may fail to respond quickly enough to unpredicted events, resulting in customer dissatisfaction. They may also spend more than is needed on fixing things that are not broken.

## 5.2.2   Communication in Service Operation (SO 3.6)

Effective communication in Service Operation ensures that all teams and departments are able to execute the standard activities involved in delivering IT services and managing the IT infrastructure.

Serious consideration should be given during Service Design to defining the content, type and format of communication that is required to operate IT services. In particular, this design needs to include:

- **Routine operational communication**: to coordinate the regular activities of Service Operation and ensure staff are aware of scheduled activities and any changes
- **Communication between shifts**: to ensure that any handover between shifts is effective

■ **Performance reporting**: IT service performance and Service Operation team or department performance

■ **Communication in projects**: to manage communication between projects and the involvement of Service Operation staff

■ **Communication related to changes**: information required to assess the impact of and successfully implement or back-out changes

■ **Communication related to exceptions**: information around any occurrence that is outside expected activity or performance

■ **Communication related to emergencies**: to allow effective investigation and management of emergency situations

■ **Communication with users and customers**: a focus on customer or user requirements and concerns.

## 5.3   PROCESSES AND ACTIVITIES

### 5.3.1   Event Management (ST 4.1) ✔

#### 5.3.1.1   Objectives ✔, scope ✘ and value ✘

Event Management provides the ability to detect events, make sense of them and determine the appropriate action. This is the entry point for many processes and can be used as the basis for automating routine operations.

The scope of Event Management includes any aspect of Service Management that needs to be controlled. This includes detecting changes in state of CIs, environmental conditions, licences and security, and can also include normal activities such as tracking application or server usage.

Event Management enables faster entry to Service Management processes, especially Incident Management, and the possibility of automating activities which deliver cost savings.

### 5.3.1.2    Basic concepts ✔

#### Definition: Event ✔

An event is a change of state which has significance for the management of a Configuration Item or IT service. The term event is also used to mean an alert or notification created by any IT service, Configuration Item or monitoring tool. Events typically require IT operations personnel to take actions, and often lead to Incidents being logged.

#### Definition: Alert ✔

An alert is a warning that a threshold has been reached, something has changed, or a failure has occurred. Alerts are often created and managed by System Management tools and are managed by the Event Management process.

Types of events include:

- **Informational:** for example, notification that a scheduled task has completed or a user has logged in
- **Warning:** typically generated when a threshold has been reached, enabling someone to react before things go wrong
- **Exception:** a service or device is operating abnormally and action is required.

### 5.3.1.3    Activities ✘

The key activities for Event Management are:

- **Event occurs**: this event may not even be detected
- **Event notification**: either the CI generates a notification or a management tool detects a status change by polling
- **Event detection**: by an agent running on the same system or a management tool
- **Event filtering**: to eliminate duplicates and unwanted events that cannot be disabled
- **Significance**: events are categorized as Informational, Warning or Exception
- **Event correlation**: a decision is made about how to proceed, based on significance of event, analysis of other related events and thresholds
- **Trigger and response selection**: all events are logged, other responses might include automated recovery, alert and human intervention, logging an incident problem or change
- **Review actions and close event**.

### 5.3.1.4    Challenges  ✗

- Obtaining funding for tools
- Setting correct level of filtering and thresholds
- Rolling out agents.

Dependency on the following critical success factors:

- Integrating Event Management into other Service Management processes
- Designing new services with Event Management in mind.

### 5.3.1.5    Key metrics  ✗

- Number of events by category, by significance, by platform and by type of event
- Number and percentage of events that required human intervention
- Number and percentage of repeat or duplicate events.

### 5.3.1.6    Roles ✗

It is unusual for an organization to appoint an 'Event Manager' as events occur in multiple contexts. Event Management roles are performed by the following Service Operation functions:

- **IT Operations Management**: monitor and respond to events for applications under their control
- **Technical and Application Management**: participate in the design and implementation of instrumentation, event classification, appropriate response, and testing; and perform Event Management for any systems and applications that have not been delegated to IT Operations
- **Service Desk**: not typically involved but may undertake a particular response such as notifying a user that a report is ready.

## 5.3.2    Incident Management (SO 4.2) ✔

### 5.3.2.1    Objectives ✔, scope ✗ and value ✗

The primary goal of Incident Management is to restore service as quickly as possible and to minimize the business impact of incidents.

The scope of Incident Management includes any event which disrupts, or could disrupt, a service.

The value of Incident Management includes:

- Detecting and resolving incidents, resulting in lower downtime to the business
- Aligning IT activity to business priorities and assigning resources as necessary
- Identification of potential improvements to services
- Identification of additional training or service requirements in IT or the business.

### 5.3.2.2    Basic concepts ✔

#### Definition: Incident ✔

An Incident is an unplanned interruption to an IT service or a reduction in the quality of an IT service. Failure of a Configuration Item that has not yet impacted service is also an Incident. For example, failure of one disk from a mirror set.

#### Definition: Impact ✔

Impact is a measure of the effect of an Incident, Problem or Change on business processes. Impact is often based on how service levels will be affected. Impact and Urgency are used to assign Priority.

#### Definition: Urgency ✔

Urgency is a measure of how long it will be until an Incident, Problem or Change has a significant Impact on the business. For example, a high Impact Incident may have low Urgency if the Impact will not affect the business until the end of the financial year. Impact and Urgency are used to assign Priority.

#### Definition: Priority ✔

Priority is a category used to identify the relative importance of an Incident, Problem or Change. Priority is based on Impact and Urgency, and is used to identify required times for actions to be taken. For example the SLA may state that Priority 2 Incidents must be resolved within 12 hours.

Incident Model

An Incident Model is a predefined way of dealing with a category of incident – for example, there may be a standard process for resolving desktop hardware problems.

### 5.3.2.3 Activities ✔

The key activities for Incident Management are:

- **Incident identification**: incidents may be detected by event management, by calls to the Service Desk, from web or other self-help interfaces, or directly by technical staff
- **Incident logging:** all incidents must be logged and time-stamped, regardless of how they are received. The log must include sufficient data to enable the incident to be managed
- **Incident categorization**: categories are used to identify the type of incident and to identify service requests so they can be passed to the request fulfilment process. Categories are also checked when the incident is closed
- **Incident prioritization**: a priority code is assigned based on impact and urgency. Priorities are dynamic and may be changed during the life of the incident
- **Initial diagnosis**: if possible the incident should be resolved while the user is on the phone. Sometimes the Service Desk Analyst will continue to work on the incident and contact the user when it has been resolved
- **Incident escalation**: 'functional escalation' is transferring the incident to a technical team with a higher level of expertise, 'hierarchic escalation' is informing or involving more senior levels of management
- **Investigation and diagnosis**: all actions taken by support groups should be recorded in the incident record
- **Resolution and recovery**: the resolution must be fully tested and documented in the incident record, before the incident is passed back to the Service Desk for closure

■ **Incident closure**: check and confirm the incident categories, carry out a user satisfaction survey, ensure all incident documentation is up to date, check to see if a problem record should be raised and then close the incident.

### 5.3.2.4   Relationships ✔

Interfaces with Incident Management include:

■ Problem Management
  - Incidents are often caused by problems
  - Incident Management may report problems
  - Problem Management prevents incidents from recurring
■ Configuration Management
  - Provides data needed to manage incidents
  - Incident Management may audit CI information
■ Change Management
  - A change may be needed to resolve an incident
  - Incidents may be caused by failed changes
■ Capacity Management
  - Incident Management may detect performance problems
  - Capacity Management may develop workarounds for incidents
■ Availability Management
  - Uses Incident Management data
■ Service Level Management
  - Agrees service levels for Incident Management
  - Reports achieved service levels for Incident Management.

### 5.3.2.5   Challenges ✘
■ Ability to detect incidents as early as possible
■ Convincing staff that all incidents must be logged
■ Availability of information about problems and known errors

■ Integration of Incident Management with the Configuration Management System and with the Service Level Management process.

Key risks to consider:

■ Having so many incidents that targets cannot be met due to lack of resources
■ Incidents not progressing due to support tools that do not raise alerts and prompt progress
■ Lack of adequate information due to inadequate tools or lack of integration
■ Mismatched objectives due to poor or non-existent OLAs and underpinning contracts.

Dependency on the following critical success factors:

■ An efficient and effective Service Desk is key to successful Incident Management
■ Clearly defined targets, as defined in SLAs
■ Adequate customer-oriented and technically trained support staff
■ Integrated support tools
■ OLAs and underpinning contracts that influence and shape behaviour of support staff.

### 5.3.2.6  Key metrics

■ Number and percentage of incidents by category, priority, time of day
■ Size of incident backlog
■ Percentage of incidents meeting required service levels for response time and resolution time, by priority and category
■ Average cost per incident by category, priority and resolution group
■ Number and percentage of incidents by Service Desk agent and resolving group.

### 5.3.2.7  Roles ✗

The following roles are needed for Incident Management:

- **Incident Manager**: drive and report on efficiency and effectiveness of the process, manage the work of incident support staff, make recommendations for improvement, manage major incidents
- **First line**: manage the initial stages in the life of an incident from logging to diagnosis, and resolve the incident if possible; escalate to second line where necessary
- **Second line**: technical support group focused on incident diagnosis and resolution
- **Third line**: deeper level of technical expertise provided by technical teams such as Network Support, Desktop Support etc.

## 5.3.3  Request Fulfilment (SO 4.3) ✔

### 5.3.3.1  Objectives ✔, scope ✗ and value ✗

The objectives of Request Fulfilment are to:

- Provide a channel for users to request and receive standard services
- Provide information about services to users and customers
- Source and deliver the components of requested standard services
- Assist with general information, complaints or comments.

The scope of Request Fulfilment is very variable. Each organization must clearly define the service requests that they will manage.

Request Fulfilment provides quick and effective access to standard services, which can lead to increased productivity for business staff and improved quality of services and products.

### 5.3.3.2    Basic concepts ✔

**Definition: Service Request ✔**

A Service Request is a request from a user for information, advice, for a standard change or for access to an IT service – for example, to reset a password or to provide standard IT services for a new user. Service Requests are usually handled by a Service Desk, and do not require an RFC to be submitted.

Most service requests are low-cost, low-risk, frequently performed changes.

### 5.3.3.3    Activities ✗

The key activities for Request Fulfilment are:

- **Menu selection**: Request Fulfilment offers great opportunities for self-help. Users should be offered a self-help menu from which they can select requests and provide details
- **Financial approval:** establish the cost of providing the service and submit this to the user for approval in their management chain
- **Other approval**: there may be a need for compliance approval, or other business agreement
- **Fulfilment**: this needs to be automated where possible, and may require OLAs and contracts with other groups. Service Desk monitors the request and keeps users informed
- **Closure**: similar to incident closure – check categorization, user satisfaction survey, update documentation, check for problems, formal closure.

### 5.3.3.4    Challenges ✗

- Clearly defining the type of requests that the process handles

■ Establishing self-help front end.

Risks to consider include:

■ Poorly defined scope
■ Poorly designed or implemented user interfaces, or fulfilment procedures
■ Inadequate monitoring.

Depends on the following critical success factors:

■ Agreement on what services are to be available, what they cost, and who may request them
■ Publication of the services as part of the Service Catalogue
■ Definition of a fulfilment procedure for each type of request.

### 5.3.3.5   Key metrics ✗
■ Mean elapsed time to handle service requests by category
■ Number and percentage of requests meeting agreed target times
■ Size of backlog and number of requests at each stage
■ Average cost by type of request
■ User satisfaction.

### 5.3.3.6   Roles ✗
Initial handling of service requests is undertaken by the Service Desk and Incident Management staff. Eventual fulfilment of the request is undertaken by the appropriate Service Operation team(s) or departments and/or by external suppliers, as appropriate.

### 5.3.4   Problem Management (SO 4.4) ✔

### 5.3.4.1   Objectives ✔, scope ✗ and value ✗
The primary objectives of Problem Management are to prevent

problems and resulting incidents from happening, to eliminate recurring incidents, and to minimize the impact of incidents that cannot be prevented.

Problem Management includes all activities needed to diagnose the root cause of incidents, and submitting change requests to resolve those problems. It also maintains information about problems and workarounds for use by Incident Management.

Effective Problem Management helps to ensure that availability and quality of services meets the business needs. It also helps to save money by reducing the number of incidents and the effort needed to resolve them. This results in less downtime for the business.

### 5.3.4.2    Basic concepts ✔

**Definition: Problem** ✔

A problem is the cause of one or more incidents. The cause is not usually known at the time a problem record is created, and the Problem Management process is responsible for further investigation.

**Definition: Workaround** ✔

A workaround is a way of reducing or eliminating the Impact of an incident or problem for which a full resolution is not yet available – for example, by restarting a failed Configuration Item. Workarounds for problems are documented in Known Error Records. Workarounds for incidents that do not have associated problem records are documented in the incident record.

### Definition: Known Error ✔

A Known Error is a problem that has a documented root cause and a workaround. Known Errors are created and managed throughout their lifecycle by Problem Management. Known Errors may also be identified by development or suppliers.

### Definition: Known Error Database ✔

A Known Error Database (KEDB) is a database containing all Known Error Records. This database is created by Problem Management and used by Incident and Problem Management. The Known Error Database is part of the Service Knowledge Management System.

### Problem Model

A Problem Model is a predefined way of dealing with a category of problem – for example, there may be a standard process for responding to intermittent server crashes.

### 5.3.4.3   Activities ✔

The key activities for Problem Management are:

- **Problem detection**: by the Service Desk, technical support, event management, notification by a supplier, or from incident trend analysis
- **Problem logging**: all details must be recorded, including links to related incidents
- **Problem categorization**: usually uses the same categorization codes as incidents

■ **Problem prioritization**: differs from incident prioritization in that this is based on frequency and impact of linked incidents, plus severity of the incident (impact on the infrastructure, cost to fix, time to fix)

■ **Problem investigation and diagnosis**: determine root cause using techniques such as chronological analysis, pain value analysis, Kepner Tregoe, brainstorming, Ishikawa diagram and Pareto analysis

■ **Workarounds**: a workaround to the related incidents can reduce the impact of the problem until full resolution is achieved

■ **Raising a Known Error Record**: for use by the Service Desk to identify the symptoms and restore service quickly, using the workaround if one exists. Create when diagnosis is complete but can be raised earlier if needed

■ **Problem resolution**: usually requires a change request. If the resolution is not cost-effective, then the problem may be left open and the workaround should continue to be used

■ **Problem closure**: after the change has been successfully reviewed – review related incident records, update Known Error Records, check problem data and formally close

■ **Major problem review**: a review of every major problem should be conducted to learn lessons for the future. Major problem is defined by the priority system.

### 5.3.4.4    Relationships

Interfaces with Problem Management include:

■ Incident Management
  - Most problems are the result of incidents
  - Incidents are often caused by problems
  - Incident Management may report problems
  - Problem Management prevents incidents from recurring
■ Change Management

- – Problem Management submits RFCs to resolve problems
- ■ Configuration Management
  - – Provides data needed to manage problems
  - – CMS can store the Known Error Database or problem records
- ■ Release and Deployment Management
  - – Deploys problem fixes
  - – Transfers development errors to the Known Error Database
  - – Problem Management resolves problems during release process
- ■ Availability Management
  - – Both processes determine how to reduce downtime
  - – Availability Management may use Problem Management data
- ■ Capacity Management
  - – Investigates capacity problems
- ■ IT Service Continuity Management
  - – Problem Management may trigger invocation of service continuity
- ■ Service Level Management
  - – Provides data needed to set Problem Management goals
  - – Occurrence of problems impacts service levels
- ■ Financial Management
  - – Provides financial data and analysis needed in decision making
  - – Problem Management provides information about cost of solutions.

## 5.3.4.5  Challenges

- ■ Linking incident and problem management tools
- ■ Relating incident and problem management records

- Working relationships between first-, second- and third-line support teams
- Understanding business impact.

Common risks to problem management are failure to address the above challenges and the following critical success factors:

- Establishment of effective Incident Management processes and tools
- Ability to use Knowledge and Configuration Management resources
- Ongoing training of technical staff.

### 5.3.4.6    Key metrics ✗

All metrics should be broken down by category, impact, severity, urgency and priority level and compared with previous periods:

- Number and percentage of problems resolved within SLA targets
- Size of backlog
- Average cost of handling problems
- Number of Known Errors added to the KEDB.

### 5.3.4.7    Roles ✗

The following roles are needed within Problem Management:

- **Problem Manager**: a single point of coordination for all Problem Management activities and an owner of the Problem Management process. The Problem Manager liaises with problem-solving groups, suppliers and contractors to ensure swift resolution of problems, and has ownership of the KEDB
- **Problem-solving groups**: technical support groups, suppliers or contractors involved in detailed problem-solving.

### 5.3.5   Access Management (SO 4.5)  ✔

#### 5.3.5.1   Objectives  ✔, scope  ✘ and value  ✘

Access Management provides the right for users to be able to use services.

Access Management helps to ensure the confidentiality, integrity and availability of data and intellectual property. It carries out activities defined in security management.

Controlled access to services helps to maintain confidentiality, and to ensure that employees have the access they need to carry out their roles. It also enables the organization to easily remove access rights when needed. Access Management provides the ability to audit use of services and to trace misuse, which may be needed for regulatory compliance.

#### 5.3.5.2   Basic concepts  ✔
- **Access:** the service functionality or data that a user is entitled to use
- **Identity:** information that distinguishes a user, each identity is unique
- **Rights:** the settings that enable a user to access a service
- **Services or service groups:** access is usually granted to groups of services, rather than to individual services
- **Directory services:** a tool that is used to manage access and rights.

#### 5.3.5.3   Activities  ✘
The key activities in Access Management are:

- **Requesting access:** this may come from an HR system, an RFC, a service request or by executing a pre-authorized script or option from a staging server. The rules for requesting access are normally documented in the service catalogue

- **Verification**: ensures that the user requesting access is who they say they are, and that they have a legitimate requirement. Usually requires independent verification
- **Providing rights**: Access Management does not decide who has access; it executes policies and regulations defined during Service Strategy and Design. It also manages requests for exceptions. Access Management often sends requests to supporting teams to actually make the changes; where possible the granting of rights should be automated
- **Monitoring identity status**: management of role changes due to job changes, promotions, transfers, resignation, death, retirement etc. The typical user lifecycle needs to be documented with tools to support the management of these changes
- **Logging and tracking access**: access monitoring and control needs to be included in all service operation functions. Exceptions are handled by Incident Management, ideally using incident models. A record of access may be needed for use in forensic investigations; this is normally provided by operations management staff, but is part of the Access Management process
- **Removing or restricting rights**: Access Management is responsible for reducing and removing access rights, as well as providing them. Rights may need to be removed after death, resignation, dismissal or transfer to a different area; rights may be restricted if the user is under investigation (but still needs some services), when the user has changed roles and needs different access, or when the user is away on a temporary basis.

### 5.3.5.4  Challenges

- Ability to verify the identity of users and approving bodies (they are who they say they are)

■ Ability to verify that a user is entitled to access a specific service
■ Ability to manage changes to a user's access requirements
■ Ability to restrict access rights
■ A database of all users and the rights they have been granted
■ Ability to link multiple rights to a user and determine the status of users.

### 5.3.5.5 Key metrics ✗

All of these metrics will typically be by service, user, department, individual granting rights etc:

■ Number of requests for access
■ Number of incidents requiring a reset of access rights
■ Number of incidents caused by incorrect access settings.

### 5.3.5.6 Roles ✗

It is unusual for an organization to appoint an 'Access Manager', although it is important that there is a single Access Management process and a single set of policies related to managing rights and access. This process and the related policies are likely to be defined and maintained by Information Security Management and executed by the various Service Operation functions as follows:

■ **Service Desk**: accept and validate requests for access to a service, pass to appropriate team to process, update user on progress
■ **Technical and Application Management**: participate in the design and implementation of access mechanisms and how abuse can be detected and stopped; assist in testing; process access requests; deal with incidents and problems
■ **IT Operations Management**: undertake any tasks delegated by Technical or Application Management.

## 5.4    PROCESSES FROM OTHER LIFECYCLE STAGES  ✗

These processes are covered in other stages of the Service Lifecycle, but there are some aspects which must be carried out by operations staff on a day-to-day basis.

### 5.4.1    Change Management (ST 4.2)  ✗

Primarily covered in Service Transition, but Service Operation staff may need to:

- Raise RFCs to address Service Operation issues
- Participate in CAB or ECAB meetings
- Implement or back out changes as directed by Change Management
- Help define change models relating to service operations
- Communicate change schedules and ensure that Service Operation staff are prepared
- Use the Change Management process for standard operational changes.

### 5.4.2    Configuration Management (ST 4.3)  ✗

Primarily covered in Service Transition, but Service Operation staff may need to:

- Inform Configuration Management of discrepancies found between CIs and the CMS
- Make changes to correct discrepancies, under the authority of Configuration Management
- Update relationships, add CIs, or change the status of CIs, as directed by Configuration Management.

### 5.4.3   Release and Deployment Management (ST 4.4)  ✗

Primarily covered in Service Transition, but Service Operation staff may need to:

- Carry out actions required to deploy new releases
- Participate in the planning of major releases
- Physically transfer CIs to and from the DML.

### 5.4.4   Capacity Management (SD 4.3)  ✗

Primarily covered in Service Design, but Service Operation staff may need to:

- Carry out daily capacity and performance monitoring, and manage thresholds; ideally this is automated as part of Event Management
- Work with event management and support groups to decide where alarms are routed and to define escalation paths and timescales
- Handle capacity and performance-related incidents
- Identify capacity and performance trends (as part of continual improvement)
- Store Capacity Management data
- Take action to implement agreed Demand Management and workload management plans.

### 5.4.5   Availability Management (SD 4.4)  ✗

Primarily covered in Service Design, but Service Operation staff may need to:

- Make the service available to the specified users at the agreed times as defined in the availability plan
- Monitor service availability
- Provide input to improvements.

### 5.4.6   Knowledge Management (ST 4.7)   ✗

Primarily covered in Service Transition, but Service Operation staff may need to:

- ▪ Provide data, metrics and information that can be used by other lifecycle stages
- ▪ Ensure that documentation such as operations manuals, procedures manuals, work instructions etc. are included in the Knowledge Management System.

### 5.4.7   Financial Management (SS 5.1)   ✗

Primarily covered in Service Strategy, but Service Operation staff may need to:

- ▪ Participate in the overall budgeting and accounting system
- ▪ Plan expenditure in good time to meet budgetary cycles
- ▪ Perform regular reviews of expenditure against budget.

### 5.4.8   IT Service Continuity Management (SD 4.5)   ✗

Primarily covered in Service Design, but Service Operation staff may need to:

- ▪ Assist in risk assessment and execute agreed risk management measures
- ▪ Assist in writing, testing and ongoing maintenance of recovery plans
- ▪ Participate in training and awareness campaigns
- ▪ Communicate with staff, customers and users during an actual disaster.

## 5.5    FUNCTIONS

Definition: Function  ✔

A function is a logical concept that refers to the people and automated measures that execute a defined process, an activity or a combination of processes or activities.

The Service Operation functions illustrated in Figure 5.1 are needed to manage the 'steady state' operational IT environment. These are logical functions that do not have to be performed by an equivalent organizational structure.

### 5.5.1    Service Desk Function (SO 6.2)  ✔

#### 5.5.1.1    Objectives  ✔, scope  ✘ and value  ✘

The Service Desk provides a single central point of contact for all users of IT. The Service Desk usually logs and manages all incidents, service requests and access requests and provides an interface for all other Service Operation processes and activities.

The primary aim of the Service Desk is to restore normal service as quickly as possible. This may involve fixing a technical fault, fulfilling a service request, or answering a query – anything that is needed to allow the users to return to normal working.

The scope of the Service Desk includes any interaction with users of IT. Responsibilities and activities include:

■ Logging all incidents and requests, categorizing and prioritizing them
■ First-line investigation and diagnosis
■ Managing the lifecycle of incidents and requests, escalating as appropriate and closing them when the user is satisfied

*Figure 5.1  Service Operation functions*

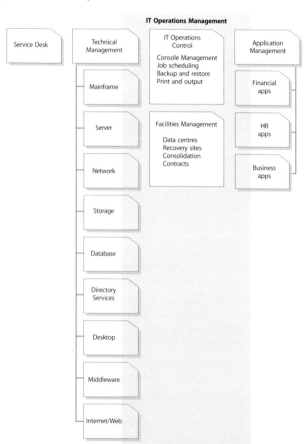

- Keeping users informed of the status of services, incidents and requests
- Conducting customer/user satisfaction callbacks/surveys
- Updating the CMS under the direction and approval of Configuration Management if so agreed.

The Service Desk is a vitally important part of an organization's IT department and is the single point of contact for IT users on a day-by-day basis. The Service Desk is key to the implementation of the Request Fulfilment and Incident Management processes described in section 5.3.

A good Service Desk is often able to compensate for deficiencies elsewhere in the IT organization, but an ineffective Service Desk can give a poor impression of an otherwise very good IT organization. It is very important that the correct calibre of staff is used on the Service Desk and that IT managers make it an attractive place to work to improve staff retention.

The benefits of a good Service Desk include:

- Improved customer service, perception and satisfaction
- Single point of contact, communication and information
- Better-quality and faster turnaround of customer or user requests
- Improved usage of IT support resources and increased productivity of users
- More meaningful management information for decision support.

### 5.5.1.2    Organizational structures (SO 6.7) ✓

There are many ways of structuring and locating Service Desks – the correct solution will vary for different organizations. The exact nature of the Service Desk should be decided by the IT department in response to customer and business requirements.

The primary options are detailed below and a combination of these may be needed in order to fully meet the business needs. Whichever combination of options is chosen, individual users need to know who to contact if they need assistance.

- **Local Service Desk**: co-located within or physically close to the user community it serves. This often aids communication, gives a clearly visible presence, and can support local language and cultural differences, but can often be inefficient and expensive to resource as the volume and arrival rate of calls may not justify the minimum staffing levels required
- **Centralized Service Desk**: the number of Service Desks can be reduced by merging them into a single location or a smaller number of locations. This can be more efficient and cost-effective, allowing fewer staff to deal with a higher volume of calls. It might still be necessary to maintain some 'local presence', but such staff can be controlled and deployed from the central desk
- **Virtual Service Desk**: through the use of technology, particularly the Internet, and corporate support tools, it is possible to give the impression of a single, centralized Service Desk when in fact the personnel may be in any number or types of locations. This gives the option of 'home working', off-shoring or outsourcing – or any combination necessary to meet user demand
- **Follow the sun**: some global or international organizations may combine two or more of their geographically dispersed Service Desks to provide a 24-hour follow-the-sun service.

This can give 24-hour coverage at relatively low cost, as no desk has to work more than a single shift. However, common processes, tools, a shared database of information, and robust handover procedures are needed for this to be successful.

### 5.5.1.3    Service Desk staffing  ✗

Call rates can be very volatile and an organization must ensure that the correct number of staff are available at any given time to match the demand being placed on the Service Desk by the business.

The following factors must be considered when deciding staffing levels:

- Customer service expectations and the number of customers and users to support, the languages they speak and their skill levels etc.
- Business requirements, such as budget, call response times, support hours, time zones etc.
- Complexity of the IT infrastructure and Service Catalogue – for example, the extent of customized versus standard off-the-shelf software deployed etc.
- The volume and type of incidents and service requests, and the responses required such as telephone, e-mail etc.
- Skill levels of staff and maturity of processes
- Supporting technologies, remote support tools, telephone etc.

The level and range of skills on the Service Desk need to be considered along with the range of options available, starting with a 'call logging' service (where staff only need basic skills) right through to a 'technical' Service Desk (where in-depth knowledge is required). The decision is often driven by target resolution times, the complexity of the systems supported and the funding available from the business.

### 5.5.1.4    Key metrics

- Percentage of calls resolved by the first line without the need for escalation
- Average time to resolve an incident (by first line)
- Average time to escalate an incident
- Average Service Desk cost of handling an incident
- Percentage of customer or user updates conducted within target service levels
- Average time to review and close a resolved call.

As well as tracking the 'hard' measures of the Service Desk's performance it is also important to assess 'soft' measures – such as how well the customers and users feel their calls have been answered. This type of measure is best obtained from the users themselves as part of a customer/user satisfaction survey.

### 5.5.1.5    Roles

The following roles are needed for the Service Desk:

- **Service Desk Manager**: take overall responsibility for the Service Desk including its role in Incident Management and Request Management; act as escalation point for supervisors; perform wider customer-services role; attend Change Advisory Board meetings
- **Service Desk Supervisor**: ensure adequate staffing and skill levels during operational hours; act as escalation point; produce statistics; assist analysts; arrange staff training and awareness sessions
- **Service Desk Analysts**: provide first-level support; handle incidents and service requests in accordance with their corresponding processes

■ **Super Users**: many organizations find it useful to designate a number of Super Users throughout the user community to act as liaison points with IT and the Service Desk. Super Users are given additional training and can filter requests and cascade information from the Service Desk outwards.

## 5.5.2    Technical Management Function (SO 6.3) ✔

### 5.5.2.1    Objectives ✔, scope ✘ and roles ✔

Technical Management helps to plan, implement and maintain a stable technical infrastructure and to ensure that required resources and expertise are in place to design, build, transition, operate and improve the IT services and supporting technology.

Technical Management includes all the people who provide technical expertise and management of the IT infrastructure.

Technical Management therefore plays a dual role:

■ The custodian of technical knowledge and expertise related to managing the IT Infrastructure
■ The actual technical resources to support the Service Lifecycle.

Technical Management is involved in two types of activity:

■ Activities that are generic to the Technical Management function as a whole, in support of managing and operating the IT services and infrastructure. These activities are summarized below
■ A set of discrete activities and processes performed by all three functions of Technical, Application and IT Operations Management, depending on the technology being managed, e.g. network and storage management.

The **generic** Technical Management activities required to manage and operate IT service and infrastructure include:

- Identifying knowledge and expertise requirements to manage and operate IT infrastructure and to deliver IT services
- Identifying skills requirements for technical staff, initiating training programmes, recruiting or contracting resources
- Design and delivery of user training
- Involvement in the design and build of new services and operational practices
- Contributing to service design, service transition or continual service improvement projects
- Assistance with Service Management processes, helping to define standards and tools, and undertaking activities such as the evaluation of change requests
- Assistance with the management of contracts and vendors.

### 5.5.2.2   Organization ✔

Technical Management is not normally provided by a single department or group. One or more Technical Support teams or departments will be needed to provide Technical Management and support for the IT infrastructure.

As illustrated in Figure 5.1, Technical Management is usually organized based on the infrastructure that each team supports, for example, mainframe team or department, storage team or department etc.

### 5.5.2.3   Key metrics ✗

Metrics for Technical Management largely depend on which technology is being managed, but some generic metric categories and examples include:

- **Measurement of agreed outputs**
  - Achievement of service levels to the business, both positive and negative, for example, the number of incidents related to a Technical Management team
  - Transaction rates and availability
  - Service level achievement
- **Process metrics:** Technical Management teams contribute to many process activities
- **Technology performance:** utilization rates of memory, availability of systems etc.
- **Mean Time Between Failures of specified equipment:** to support purchasing decisions and effectiveness of maintenance
- **Measurement of maintenance activity:** for example, number of maintenance windows exceeded
- **Training and skills development**.

### 5.5.2.4   Roles ✔

The following roles are needed within Technical Management:

- **Technical Managers/Team leaders**: take overall responsibility for leadership, control, decision making and line management for the technical team or department; ensure technical competence, training and awareness
- **Technical Analysts/Architects**: work with users and other stakeholders to determine their needs; define and maintain knowledge of systems and relationships; perform cost-benefit analyses; define operational model and tasks
- **Technical Operators**: staff who perform day-to-day operational tasks within Technical Management, usually delegated to the IT Operations team.

### 5.5.3 IT Operations Management Function (SO 6.4) ✔

#### 5.5.3.1 Objectives ✔, scope ✘ and roles ✔

IT Operations Management is responsible for performing the day-to-day operational activities required to manage and maintain the IT infrastructure and deliver the agreed level of IT services to the business.

The objectives of IT Operations Management include:

- Achieving stability of the organization's day-to-day processes and activities
- Continual improvement to achieve improved service at reduced costs, while maintaining stability
- Rapid diagnosis and resolution of any IT operations failures that occur.

IT Operations Management includes two functions:

- **IT Operations Control**: staffed by shifts of operators who carry out routine operational tasks. They provide centralized monitoring and control, usually from an operations bridge or network operations centre. Specific activities include:
    - Console management – defining and operating a central observation and monitoring capability
    - Job scheduling – the management of routine batch jobs or scripts
    - Backup and restore – on behalf of all Technical and Application Management teams and departments and often on behalf of users
    - Print and output management
    - Maintenance activities – on behalf of Technical or Application Management teams or departments

■ **Facilities Management**: responsible for the management of data centres, computer rooms and recovery sites together with their power and cooling requirements. Facilities Management also coordinates large-scale projects, such as data centre consolidation or server consolidation.

### 5.5.3.2    Organization ✔

As illustrated in Figure 5.1, IT Operations Management is often seen as a function in its own right, but in many cases, staff from Technical and Application Management groups form part of this function. There is no single method for assigning activities; some Technical and Application Management departments or groups manage and execute their own operational activities, whilst others delegate these activities to a dedicated IT Operations department.

### 5.5.3.3    Key metrics ✘

■ IT Operations Control
  – Number of exceptions to scheduled activities and jobs
  – Number of data or system restores
  – Equipment implementation, number of items, success etc.
  – Process metrics – IT Operations Management contributes to many process activities.

■ Facilities Management
  – Number of incidents related to the buildings, power and cooling etc.
  – Number of security incidents
  – Power usage statistics.

### 5.5.3.4    Roles ✔

The following roles are needed within IT Operations Management:

- ■ **IT Operations Manager**: takes overall responsibility for leadership, control, decision making and line management for the IT Operations Management teams or department
- ■ **Shift Leaders**: many IT Operations areas work extended hours on either a two- or three-shift basis. Shift Leaders must:
  - – take overall responsibility for the shift period
  - – ensure operational duties are successfully completed within agreed timescales
  - – manage shift handover
  - – manage Operations Analysts
- ■ **Operations Analysts**: senior IT Operations staff able to determine the most effective and efficient way to conduct a series of operations, e.g. job scheduling, definition of backup and restore schedules
- ■ **IT Operators**: staff who perform day-to-day operational activities such as performing backups, console operations, scheduled housekeeping jobs etc.

### 5.5.4    Application Management Function (SO 6.5)  ✔

#### 5.5.4.1    Objectives  ✔, scope  ✗ and roles  ✔

Application Management is responsible for managing applications throughout their lifecycle. Application Management also plays an important role in the design, testing and improvement of applications that form part of IT services. Application Management may therefore be involved in development projects, but is not usually the same as the Applications Development teams.

Application Management includes all the people who provide technical expertise and management of applications. In this respect, they carry out a very similar role to Technical Management, but with a focus on software applications rather than infrastructure.

Application Management therefore plays a dual role:

- Being the custodian of technical knowledge and expertise related to managing applications
- Providing the actual application resources to support the Service Lifecycle.

It is common in many organizations to refer to applications as services, but applications are just one component needed to provide a service. Each application may support more than one service, and each service may make use of many applications. This is especially true for modern service providers who create shared services based on service-oriented architectures.

Application Management works closely with Development, but is a distinct function with different roles. Activities carried out by Application Management are similar to those described above for Technical Management.

### 5.5.4.2  Basic concepts  ✗

- **Build or buy**: One of the key decisions in Application Management during the Service Design stage is whether to buy an application that supports the required functionality, or whether to build the application specifically for the organization's requirements
- **Operational models**: the specification of the operational environment in which the application runs when it goes live. This is also used during testing and transition phases to simulate and evaluate the live environment
- **Application Management lifecycle**: the lifecycle followed to develop and manage applications as defined in a number of formal approaches, which includes the steps shown in Figure 5.2. This Application Management lifecycle is complementary to and matches the ITIL Service Management lifecycle.

*Figure 5.2 Application Management lifecycle*

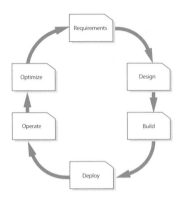

### 5.5.4.3  Activities

- Identifying the knowledge and expertise required
- Identifying skills requirements for technical staff, initiating training programmes, recruiting or contracting resources
- Design and delivery of user training
- Definition of standards for the design of new architectures
- Involvement in the design and building of new services
- Managing application vendors
- Definition of Event Management standards
- Problem Management
- Support of other Service Management processes.

### 5.5.4.4  Organization

Application Management is usually organized along the lines of business that each team supports such as Financial applications, Messaging and Collaboration applications, HR applications etc.

### 5.5.4.5    Key metrics ✗

Metrics for Application Management largely depend on which applications are being managed, but some generic metric categories and examples include:

- **Measurement of agreed outputs**
    - Ability of users to access applications
    - Reports and files transmitted to users in accordance with service levels
    - Transaction rates achieved

- **Process metrics**: Application Management teams contribute to many process activities
- **Application performance**: response times, availability of systems, data integrity etc.
- **Measurement of maintenance activity**: for example, number of maintenance windows exceeded
- **Training and skills development.**

### 5.5.4.6    Roles ✔

The following roles are needed within Application Management:

- **Application Managers/Team leaders**: take overall responsibility for leadership, control, decision making and line management for the technical team or department; ensure technical competence, training and awareness
- **Applications Analysts/Architects**: work with users and other stakeholders to determine their needs; perform cost-benefit analyses; develop optimal operational models and tasks; develop and maintain standards.

# 6 Continual Service Improvement

Continual Service Improvement is responsible for managing improvements to IT Service Management Processes and IT services. The performance of the IT service provider is continually measured and improvements are made to processes, IT services and IT infrastructure in order to increase efficiency, effectiveness and cost-effectiveness.

## 6.1 GOALS, OBJECTIVES, SCOPE AND VALUE (CSI 2.4)

### 6.1.1 Goals ✔

Continual Service Improvement (CSI) aims to deliver business value by focusing on the realization of benefits from implementation of the Service Lifecycle approach.

### 6.1.2 Objectives ✔

CSI has the following objectives:

- Review, analyse and make recommendations on improvement opportunities in each lifecycle stage
- Review and analyse service level achievement results
- Identify and implement individual activities to improve service quality and the efficiency and effectiveness of Service Management processes
- Improve cost-effectiveness of delivering IT services without sacrificing customer satisfaction
- Ensure applicable quality management methods are used to support continual improvement activities.

CSI must be an objective for everyone in the organization, but improvement activities don't just happen. Responsibility for ensuring that CSI is implemented throughout the organization and across all lifecycle stages should be given to a senior responsible owner who possesses the appropriate authority to make things happen.

Improvement activities need to be planned and scheduled on an ongoing basis. Ideally 'improvement' will become a process in its own right, carried out at all levels throughout the organization.

### 6.1.3   Scope   ✗

CSI is applicable across all stages of the Service Lifecycle and seeks to continually improve the services delivered to support and enable business processes. It addresses three main areas:

- Overall health of Service Management as a discipline
- Continual alignment of the portfolio with current and future business needs
- Maturity of the enabling IT processes.

### 6.1.4   Value to business (CSI 2.4.5)   ✗

CSI recognizes that the value it provides to the business can be realized and measured in different ways:

- Improvements: outcomes that are favourably improved when compared to a 'before' state
- Benefits: the gains achieved through realization of improvements
- ROI: the difference between the benefit and the cost to achieve it
- VOI: the extra value created by the establishment of benefits that include non-monetary outcomes.

Implementing CSI implies ongoing investment to create and maintain Service Improvement Plans (SIPs).

CSI ensures that focus on the value delivered on an investment is not only applied up-front, in the creation of a Business Case to help to secure the investment, it also places emphasis on the need for periodic re-evaluation after implementation of the improvement:

- Checking year-by-year benefits/ROI/VOI are realized by specific improvements
- Identifying best-value investments by estimating benefits from competing initiatives
- Assessing the impact on current benefit by:
  - A proposed organizational change
  - A change in business strategy
  - Regulatory or legislative change.

## 6.2 KEY PRINCIPLES

### 6.2.1 The Deming Cycle – Plan, Do, Check, Act (CSI 3.6, 5.5.1) ✔

The Deming Cycle (Plan, Do, Check, Act – PDCA Model) is widely used as the foundation for quality improvement activities across many types of organization.

It forms the foundation of most other successful improvement approaches and techniques.

- **Plan**: clearly document the target state and the intended steps to get there
- **Do**: execute the plan
- **Check**: monitor and measure outcomes to determine actual achievements against the plan
- **Act**: identify gaps against expectations and opportunities for further improvement.

Following each pass through the cycle there is a phase of consolidation to ensure the improvement is embedded and that the benefits achieved will not begin to be lost.

## 6.2.2 Continual Service Improvement model (CSI 2.4.4) ✔

*Figure 6.1 Continual Service Improvement model*

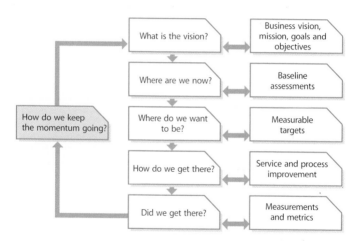

The Continual Service Improvement model (see Figure 6.1) illustrates the need for a constant cycle of improvement. The model consists of six steps:

- Clarify the vision, taking into account business and IT vision, mission, goals and objectives
- Assess the current situation, using baseline assessments
- Determine the priorities for improvement, setting measurable targets

- Document an improvement plan, using service and process improvement techniques
- Monitor achievements, making use of appropriate measures and metrics
- Maintain momentum by ensuring improvements are embedded, and through continual re-evaluation.

### 6.2.3 Metrics, Key Performance Indicators and measurement (CSI 4.1.2) ✔

Metric

A metric is something that is measured and reported to help manage a process, IT service or activity. Metrics drive what is to be measured. For instance, a 'cost' metric will drive the measurement of a number of specific cost drivers such as people, facilities or parts.

Key Performance Indicator

A Key Performance Indicator (KPI) is a metric that is used to help manage a process, IT service or activity. Many metrics may be measured, but only the most important of these are defined as KPIs and used to actively manage and report on the process, IT service or activity. KPIs should be selected to ensure that efficiency, effectiveness and cost-effectiveness are all managed.

Measurement

Appropriate KPIs and other metrics should be selected and used to measure whether IT services, processes and activities are meeting their goals and objectives. This data can then be analysed to identify improvement opportunities and optimize efficiency and effectiveness.

There are three types of metric that an organization may collect to support CSI:

- **Technology metrics**: often associated with components and applications
- **Process metrics**: to help to determine the overall health of a process
- **Service metrics**: the results of the delivery of end-to-end service.

Tension metrics make use of two or more metrics to help ensure balance. Activities which improve one metric can make another worse. Such metrics should be analysed together to help drive the required behaviour.

## 6.2.4   IT governance across the Service Lifecycle (CSI 3.10) ✔

### Definition: Governance ✔

Governance ensures that policies and strategy are actually implemented, and that required processes are correctly followed. Governance includes defining roles and responsibilities, measuring and reporting, and taking actions to resolve any issues identified.

Enterprise governance covers the concepts of both corporate and business governance:

- Corporate governance focuses on conformance to (usually external) regulatory or legislative frameworks and standards
- Business governance measures performance against the vision, mission and goals of the organization in line with internal policies and procedures.

IT governance is an integral part of enterprise governance and consists of the leadership, organizational structures and processes which ensure that the organization's IT sustains and extends the organization's strategy and objectives.

These different forms of governance do not operate in isolation and together serve to demonstrate:

- Accountability
- Value creation
- Assurance
- Resource utilization.

The principles of the Service Lifecycle ensure services are created to deliver business value by recognizing business objectives while taking into account the demands and constraints imposed by legal and regulatory requirements. IT governance acts across the Service Lifecycle to ensure appropriate policies, procedures, processes and measurements are in place and that they are implemented and adhered to.

## 6.3   PROCESSES AND ACTIVITIES

### 6.3.1   7-Step Improvement Process (CSI 4.1) ✘

#### 6.3.1.1   Objectives ✘, scope ✘ and value ✘

The objectives of the 7-Step Improvement Process are to:

- Identify and develop a set of measures that are relevant to business requirements and which will support the identification of effective improvement opportunities
- Adopt a structured approach to gathering, processing and analysing that data in order to identify improvement opportunities
- Communicate those improvement opportunities effectively to allow decisions to be made on next steps.

The 7-Step Improvement Process is fundamental in supporting CSI and operates across the entire Service Lifecycle. It focuses on identifying improvement opportunities, not only for the processes and services, but also for the disciplines implemented as part of each of the lifecycle stages – including the discipline of CSI itself.

Value is created through a constant focus on the application of the principles of the Service Lifecycle, the delivery of services, and on the processes implemented with a view to ensuring they continue to align with, and deliver against, business requirements and to identify opportunities for continual improvement.

### 6.3.1.2    Basic concepts ✗

- Measures must be derived from business requirements, linked to goals and objectives
- Measure only what will be useful in demonstrating achievement of goals and in identifying improvement opportunities
- Constantly review measures for relevance and applicability and discard those that are not
- Analyse the data and present information in a way that is useful to the intended audience.

### 6.3.1.3    Activities ✗

***Figure 6.2  7-Step Improvement Process***

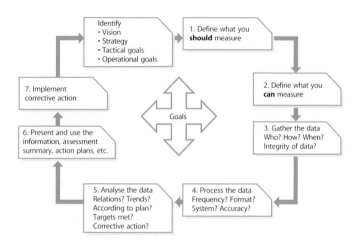

## Step one – Define what you should measure

Take into account vision, strategy, goals and objectives to determine what to measure. These measurements should enable the provider to demonstrate value to the business by linking back through to key business drivers.

## Step two – Define what you can measure

Take into account the current capabilities of tools and processes to provide the measurements identified in step one. Conduct a gap analysis and determine if up-front work is needed to be able to measure what is required.

### Step three – Gather the data

Use monitoring to gather the data. Monitoring may be either automatic or manual. Consistency within a data set can be assured where the data is gathered automatically, so where it is carried out manually, additional controls should be implemented such as policies, standards and procedures.

### Step four – Process the data

Convert the data gathered into the required format for the audience. This can be seen as converting the metrics into KPI results, turning data into information.

### Step five – Analyse the data

Transform the information, combining results from different areas, into knowledge. Develop an understanding of the real meaning of identified patterns and trends. Answer questions such as:

- Is this good or bad? Why?
- Is this expected and in line with targets? If not, why not?

### Step six – Present and use the information

Communicate the information at the right level of detail for the audience and in a way that is understandable, provides value and supports informed decision making.

### Step seven – Implement corrective action

Use the knowledge gained to optimize, improve and correct services across the entire Service Lifecycle.

#### 6.3.1.4    Challenges ✗

There are some challenges for management, so it is advisable to remember the following:

- Don't try to do too much too soon; start simply and ensure the focus is on measuring the right things

- Try to justify investment up-front to ensure the organization can measure what it should measure
- Ensure manual data collection is being carried out accurately and consistently. Manually capturing data on how a process was carried out and what the outcome was can be seen as an administrative overhead. Ongoing communication about the benefits of performing these tasks is essential.

### 6.3.1.5    Key metrics ✗

- Increased number of CSI-driven process and service improvement opportunities identified
- Increased number of improvements to the Capacity and Availability Plans as a result of the identification of what will be measured
- Increased understanding and use of the reports and the underlying meaning of trends and patterns
- Improved customer satisfaction measurement results.

### 6.3.1.6    Organization and roles (CSI 6.1) ✗

There are various key roles that are essential to the effective implementation of this process for CSI. In particular:

- **Reporting Analyst:** responsibilities include:
  - Ensuring the validity of the reporting metrics
  - Consolidating data from multiple sources
  - Identifying trends and analysing the underlying meaning of the trend
  - Producing reports on service performance.

- **CSI Manager:** responsibilities include:
  - Communicating the vision of CSI across the organization
  - Working with the Service Owner to identify and prioritize improvement opportunities

- Working with the Service Level Manager to ensure that monitoring requirements are defined and to identify Service Improvement Plans
- Identifying frameworks, models and standards that will support CSI activities
- Ensuring that CSI activities are coordinated throughout the entire Service Lifecycle
- Presenting improvement recommendations to senior management.

CSI is implemented at all stages of the Service Lifecycle. It interfaces with all processes and most roles.

The most significant process interface is with the Service Level Management process:

- To document and agree SLA targets that are used to identify what should and could be measured
- To assist with the analysis and interpretation of the output of monitoring activities
- To agree and drive Service Improvement Plans (SIPs).

The most significant role interfaces are:

- Service Level Manager
- Service Owner
- Process Owner
- Service Manager.

## 6.3.2 Service Reporting (CSI 4.2)

### 6.3.2.1 Objectives, scope and value

The objective of Service Reporting is to deliver the right content to the right audience. A significant amount of data is collected, but only a small subset is of interest to the business. The majority is more suited to internal management.

Reporting that focuses on the future as strongly as the past also provides a means to market IT services that are directly aligned to the positive or negative experiences of the business.

### 6.3.2.2 Basic concepts ✗

Reporting policy and rules

Take time to define and agree the policy and rules with the business and Service Design Manager about how reporting will be implemented and managed, including:

- Targeted audience and related business views on the service delivered
- Agreement on what to measure, what to report, definitions of all terms and boundaries, and the basis of all calculations
- Reporting schedules
- Access to reports and the medium to be used
- Meetings scheduled to review and discuss reports.

### 6.3.2.3 Activities ✗

The key activities of Service Reporting are:

- Define reporting policies and rules
- Collate data
- Translate into meaningful business views and apply to report templates
- Publish in agreed mediums
- Review with business.

### 6.3.2.4 Challenges ✗

- Avoiding reports which only depict adherence to SLAs, building a proactive actionable approach to reporting
- Balancing simple automated standardized reporting with more meaningful customized reports
- Keeping language and content unambiguous, meaningful and relevant.

### 6.3.2.5 Key metrics ✗

As agreed with the business, depending on the contracted service and SLAs, including:

- ■ Representation of past performance
- ■ Future mitigation of past issues
- ■ Future improvements.

### 6.3.2.6 Roles ✗

As described in section 6.3.1.6.

### 6.3.3 Service Measurement (CSI 4.3) ✗

Whilst knowledge of the Service Measurement process is not required for the ITIL Foundation exam, some specific concepts are required and these are indicated with a ✔.

### 6.3.3.1 Objectives ✗, scope ✗ and value ✗

Service Measurement aims to establish a measurement framework which measures not only at individual component level, but is also able to consolidate and provide measures for end-to-end services and at multiple levels across services.

Service Measurement includes supplier performance.

Service Measurement provides value to the business by enabling it to:

- ■ Validate previous decisions
- ■ Set direction in order to hit targets
- ■ Justify that a course of action is required
- ■ Intervene and to take corrective action.

Service Measurements need to be continually re-evaluated to ensure they remain relevant and useful.

### 6.3.3.2    Basic concepts ✔
Baselines (CSI 3.7.1)

An important starting point for any improvement activity is establishing a baseline. A baseline is a benchmark that can be used as a reference point. For example, an ITSM baseline can be used as a starting point to measure the effect of a Service Improvement Plan; a performance baseline can be used to measure changes in performance over the lifetime of an IT service; a Configuration Management baseline can be used to enable the IT infrastructure to be restored to a known configuration if a change or release fails.

It is essential to collect baseline data at the outset, even if the integrity of the data is in question. It is better to have baseline data to question than to have no baseline data at all.

### 6.3.3.3    Activities ✘
The key activities for Service Measurement are:

- Develop a Service Measurement framework and choose measures
    - Identify critical business processes
    - Determine which services, components, processes, activities and outputs need to be monitored
- Define procedures and policies to support service measurement, including tools to be used
- Interpret and use metrics, e.g. to make decisions, or for comparison against norms or targets
- Create scorecards and reports for the business, IT management and IT operational/technical management.

### 6.3.3.4  Challenges  ✗

- Creation of a service measurement framework that leads to value-added reporting
- Selecting a measurement framework that is balanced and unbiased, and able to withstand change
- Avoiding the mistake of creating and distributing the same reports to everyone.

### 6.3.3.5  Key metrics  ✗

Ensure measures are in place to support:

- Service performance against strategic business and IT plans
- Risk and compliance
- Business contribution – showing how IT supports the business
- Key IT processes
- Internal and external customer satisfaction.

### 6.3.3.6  Roles  ✗

As described in section 6.3.1.6.

## 6.4    ADDITIONAL ORGANIZATION ROLES  ✓

For CSI to be successful, specific roles and responsibilities need to be defined across the Service Lifecycle, and as these change over time these roles need to be redefined and responsibilities reallocated.

### 6.4.1  Roles (CSI 6.1)  ✓

Responsibility for each process and service must be clear to ensure effective delivery.

The two key generic roles are Process Owner and Service Owner. They do not have to be carried out by a dedicated person, and the responsibilities of each role may be combined with other organizational roles, depending on the size and volatility of the organization. It is important that the roles, responsibilities, processes, dependencies and interfaces are clearly defined and scoped.

■ **Process Owner** ✔: responsible for ensuring that all activities within a process are undertaken and responsible for:
  – Defining the process strategy
  – Assisting with process design
  – Ensuring process documentation is available and current
  – Auditing to ensure compliance.

The Process Owner role is relevant across the lifecycle. Process and role interfaces for the Process Owner are driven by the relevant process.

■ **Service Owner** ✔: answerable for a particular service with the responsibility for:
  – Acting as the prime contact for all service-related enquiries and issues
  – Ensuring that the service is delivered to agreed service levels
  – Identifying opportunities for service improvements
  – Facilitating effective service monitoring.

The Service Owner retains responsibility for the service across the lifecycle. This role interfaces with all processes and the related roles.

## 6.4.2  Authority matrix (CSI 6.2)  ✔

An authority matrix is often used within organizations to indicate roles and responsibilities in relation to processes and activities.

The **RACI model** is an example of an authority matrix. It is used to map the activities related to a process to the roles involved in their execution. The acronym RACI is derived from the distinct ways a role can be involved in a process or activity:

- **R**esponsible: executes the process or activity *(does the work)*
- **A**ccountable: ownership of quality and end result *(ultimate owner)*
- **C**onsulted: input of knowledge and information *(provides assistance)*
- **I**nformed: receives information about execution *(needs to know)*.

Within the RACI model, each activity must have someone identified for R and A, whereas C and I are optional. Only one person can be Accountable for each activity.

Generic roles are normally used in the RACI model, but it is vitally important that the Role-to-Activity links it describes are mapped back to the real organization.

Separating the RACI from the organization allows flexibility in the application of Role-Activity relationships to the realities and constraints of organizational design:

- It recognizes that the same process or activity may be carried out by more than one organizational role or unit
- It allows organization design to change without impacting the underlying process model
- It recognizes constraints of geographically diverse organizations, which may have to combine many responsibilities in fewer roles on smaller sites
- It allows for complex organizations covering diverse businesses to adopt the same underlying process model without extensive adaptation.

# 7 Qualifications    *x*

## 7.1 OVERVIEW

The ITIL v3 Qualifications Scheme has four levels:

- Foundation level
- Intermediate level (Lifecycle and Capability streams)
- ITIL Expert
- ITIL Master.

Candidates gain credits for each examination taken, leading to an ITIL Expert certificate (22 credits). The ITIL Master certificate is in development.

*Figure 7.1 ITIL v3 Qualifications Scheme*

## 7.2 FOUNDATION

The Foundation level ensures candidates gain knowledge of the ITIL terminology, structure and basic concepts, and comprehend the core principles of ITIL practices for Service Management. Foundation represents 2 credits towards the ITIL Expert.

## 7.3    INTERMEDIATE LEVEL

There are two streams in the Intermediate level, assessing an individual's ability to analyse and apply concepts of ITIL:

- Lifecycle stream
- Capability stream.

**Lifecycle stream** – built around the five core publications for candidates wanting to gain knowledge within the Service Lifecycle context. Each module achieves 3 credits.

**Capabilities stream** – built around four practitioner-based clusters for candidates wanting to gain knowledge around specific processes and roles. Each module achieves 4 credits:

- **Planning, protection and optimization**: including capacity, availability, continuity, security, demand and risk management
- **Service offerings and agreement**: including portfolio, service level, catalogue, demand, supplier and financial management
- **Release, control and validation**: including change, release and deployment, validation and testing, service asset and configuration, knowledge, request management and evaluation
- **Operational support and analysis**: including event, incident, request, problem, access, Service Desk, Technical, IT Operations and Application Management.

Candidates may take units from either of the streams to accumulate credits.

To complete the Intermediate level, the Managing across the Lifecycle course (5 credits) is required to bring together the full essence of a lifecycle approach to Service Management, consolidating knowledge gained across the qualifications scheme.

## 7.4   ITIL EXPERT

Candidates automatically qualify for an ITIL Expert certificate once they have achieved the pre-requisite 22 credits from Foundation (mandatory initial unit) and Intermediate units (including Managing across the Lifecycle, mandatory final unit). No further examination or courses are required.

## 7.5   ITIL MASTER

Although not yet finalized, this qualification is intended to assess an individual's ability to apply and analyse the ITIL v3 concepts in new areas.

## 7.6   EXISTING ITIL V1 AND V2 QUALIFICATIONS

*Figure 7.2  ITIL v3 bridging qualification scheme*

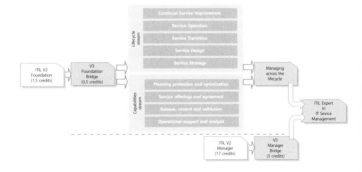

The ITIL v3 scheme has bridging courses for those candidates with existing ITIL (v1 and v2) qualifications. An existing ITIL v1 or v2 Foundation qualification equates to 1.5 credits, and successfully passing a v3 Foundation Bridge course provides the further 0.5 credits required to progress to the Intermediate level.

A v1 or v2 Manager qualification equates to 17 credits and successfully passing a v3 Manager Bridge course provides the further 5 credits required to achieve the ITIL Expert certificate.

There are also credits for the v2 practitioners, either 2 credits for single processes or 3.5 for clustered processes.

ITIL provides advice and guidance on best practice relating to the provision of IT services. The following public frameworks and standards are relevant:

- ISO/IEC 20000: IT Service Management
- ISO/IEC 27001: Information Security Management (ISO/IEC 17799 is the corresponding Code of Practice)
- ISO/IEC 14001: Environmental Management
- ISO/IEC 15504 (SPICE)
- ISO/IEC 19770 (Software Asset Management)
- ISO/IEC 38500 (Governance)
- Capability Maturity Model Integration (CMMI®)
- Control Objectives for Information and related Technology (COBIT®)
- Projects in Controlled Environments (PRINCE2™)
- Project Management Body of Knowledge (PMBOK®)
- Management of Risk (M_o_R®)
- eSourcing Capability Model for Service Providers (eSCM-SP™)
- Telecom Operations Map (eTOM®)
- Six Sigma™.

Organizations need to integrate guidance from multiple frameworks and standards.

The primary standard for IT Service Management is ISO/IEC 20000. The standard and ITIL are aligned and continue to be aligned, although the standard is currently to be extended with the development of Parts 3 and 4:

- ISO/IEC 20000-1:2005 Part 1: Specification (Defines the requirements for Service Management)

- ISO/IEC 20000-2:2005 Part 2: Code of Practice (Provides guidance and recommendations on how to meet the requirements in Part 1)
- ISO/IEC 20000-3:2007 Part 3: Scoping and applicability (Not available yet)
- ISO/IEC 20000-4:2007 Part 4: Service Management Process Reference Model (Not available yet)
- BIP 0005: A Manager's Guide to Service Management
- BIP 0015 IT Service Management: Self-assessment Workbook (currently assesses against ITIL v2, to be revised via ITIL v3 complementary publications).

These documents provide a standard against which organizations can be assessed and certified with regard to the quality of their IT Service Management processes.

An ISO/IEC 20000 Certification scheme was introduced in December 2005. The scheme was designed by the itSMF UK and is operated under their control. A number of auditing organizations are accredited within the scheme to assess and certify organizations as compliant to the ISO/IEC 20000 standard and its content.

# Further guidance and contact points

## TSO

PO Box 29
Norwich NR3 1GN
United Kingdom
Tel: +44(0) 870 600 5522
Fax: +44(0) 870 600 5533
E-mail: customer.services@tso.co.uk
www.tso.co.uk

## OGC

Rosebery Court
St Andrews Business Park
Norwich NR7 0HS
United Kingdom
Tel: +44(0) 845 000 4999
E-mail: ServiceDesk@ogc.gsi.gov.uk
www.itil.co.uk

## itSMF LTD

150 Wharfedale Road
Winnersh Triangle
Wokingham
Berkshire RG41 5RB
United Kingdom
Tel: +44(0) 118 918 6500
Fax: +44(0) 118 969 9749
E-mail: service@itsmf.co.uk
www.itsmf.co.uk

## APM GROUP LTD

Sword House
Totteridge Road
High Wycombe
Buckinghamshire HP13 6DG
United Kingdom
Tel: +44(0) 1494 452 450
Fax: +44(0) 1494 459 559
E-mail: servicedesk@apmgroup.co.uk
www.apmgroup.co.uk

## BEST PRACTICE WITH ITIL

The ITIL V3 publication portfolio consists of a unique library of titles that offer guidance on quality IT services and best practices.

*The ITIL Lifecycle Suite* (core publications)

- *Service Strategy*
- *Service Design*
- *Service Transition*
- *Service Operation*
- *Continual Service Improvement*

*Introduction to the ITIL Service Lifecycle*

*Key Element Guides* (pocket-sized reference books based on the core publications)

*Passing your ITIL Foundation Exam* (the official ITIL Foundation study aid)

*An Introductory Overview of ITIL V3* (co-branded with itSMF UK)

*ITIL V3 Foundation Handbook (co-branded with itSMF UK)*

## ABOUT itSMF

The itSMF is the only truly independent and internationally recognized forum for IT Service Management professionals worldwide. This not-for-profit organization is a prominent player in the ongoing development and promotion of IT Service Management best practice, standards and qualifications, and has been since 1991.

Globally, the itSMF now boasts over 6,000 member companies, blue-chip and public-sector alike, covering in excess of 70,000 individuals spread over 40+ international chapters.

Each chapter is a separate legal entity and is largely autonomous. itSMF International provides an overall steering and support function to existing and emerging chapters. It has its own website at www.itsmfi.org

The UK chapter has over 16,000 members: it offers a flourishing annual conference, online bookstore, regular regional meetings and special interest groups and numerous other benefits for members. Its website is at www.itsmf.co.uk.

## ABOUT THE BEST MANAGEMENT PRACTICE PARTNERSHIP

### UK government and best practice

The Office of Government Commerce (OGC), as an office of HM Treasury, plays a vital role in developing methodologies, processes and frameworks and establishing these as best practice.

The huge growth in the market for OGC's best-practice guidance is evidence of how highly it is valued – proving that it offers not just theory but workable business solutions. ITIL is now the most widely accepted approach to Service Management in the world, while PRINCE2 has established itself as a global leader in project management.

OGC, on behalf of the UK government, remains committed to maintaining and developing the guidance. Through an innovative and successful partnering arrangement, OGC is able to ensure that users are supported by high-quality publications, training, qualification schemes and consultancy services.

OGC and its official partners

In 2006, OGC completed an open competitive procurement and appointed The Stationery Office (TSO) as official publisher and the APM Group Ltd (APMG) as official accreditor. Together they have created the Best Management Practice, as the official home of OGC's best-practice guidance. The partners are committed to delivering, supporting and endorsing the very best products and services in the market place.

**The Stationery Office (TSO)**

TSO draws upon over 200 years of print and publishing services experience, and is the only official publisher for OGC's best-practice guidance.

TSO also manages the various refresh projects on OGC's behalf and ensures that the quality of the guidance is maintained at the highest possible level. A dedicated team serves the Best Management Practice community, providing newsletters, updates and latest information on the products and current projects.

**APM Group (APMG)**

APMG is a global business providing accreditation and certification services. It is one of the first medium-sized companies to establish an independent Ethics and Standards Board to monitor its business practice and to help ensure it supports the industries it serves in a transparent and responsible way.

APMG has been instrumental in helping to establish PRINCE2 as an international standard and now provides global accreditation schemes in ITIL, PRINCE2, MSP™ (Managing Successful Programmes) and M_o_R (Management of Risk).

Keep up to date with best management practice

The Best Management Practice Knowledge Centre brings together the official partners and recognized user groups to create a comprehensive source of information. Here you can find articles, white papers, book reviews and events, as well as links to the individual product sites.

Visit www.best-management-practice.com